HISTORY
OF GRAPHIC DESIGN
AND COMMUNICATION

HISTORY
OF GRAPHIC DESIGN
AND COMMUNICATION

A SOURCE BOOK

compiled by
CLIVE ASHWIN
BA ARCM CertEd
AcDipEd MPhil PhD

Pembridge HISTORY OF DESIGN *Series*
Editors: PETER GREEN and DAVID F CHESHIRE

 PEMBRIDGE PRESS

First published 1983

ISBN: 0-82606-005-2

Typeset by Allset Composition in 11 on 13 point Baskerville

CONTENTS

ACKNOWLEDGEMENTS
PAGE ix

INTRODUCTION
PAGE 1

SOURCES

ACKNOWLEDGEMENTS

I have made use of several libraries in the course of preparing this source book, and I should like to express my gratitude to the staff of the following for their assistance: the Library of the Faculty of Art and Design, Middlesex Polytechnic; the National Art Library, Victoria and Albert Museum; the St Bride Printing Library.

I am grateful to the following for having given me permission to reproduce extracts from the publications cited: to J. M. Dent & Sons Ltd, in respect of Eric Gill *An essay on typography*; to Cambridge University Press, in respect of Stanley Morison *First principles of typography*; to Frau Edith Tschichold, in respect of Jan Tschichold *Die neue Typographie*; to Bruckmann, München and *Novum Gebrauchsgraphik*, in respect of *Gebrauchsgraphik*; to Professor G. W. Ovink, in respect of G. W. Ovink *Legibility, atmosphere-value and forms of printing types*; to Houghton Mifflin Company, in respect of Harold Ernest Burtt *The psychology of advertising*; to the Orthological Institute in respect of Otto Neurath *International picture language*; to M. Jacques Bertin and Mouton Editeur, in respect of Jacques Bertin *Sémiologie graphique*. I have been unable to trace the present owners of copyright in Edmund J. Sullivan *The art of illustration*.

I am very grateful to Mrs Henriette Fishlock, Mrs Philippa Sutherland and Dr Roy Armes for reading my translations and for making several helpful suggestions for revisions.

The purpose of this book is to bring together in one convenient volume a collection of sources which reflect major developments in the history of graphic design and graphic communication since about 1800. The expression 'graphic design' is not in itself sufficient to denote the full range of sources used, since for most of the period in question there was no identifiable professional activity or industrial role which could be described as 'graphic design' in the contemporary sense, nor a class of person known as a 'graphic designer' in the sense of someone responsible for coordinating all the ingredients of *genres* of graphic communication such as books, periodicals, handbills, posters, tickets, and other ephemera.

All artefacts, however primitive, may be said to have been designed, albeit with varying degrees of deliberateness, skill and success: although he did not produce measured drawings, stone-age man 'designed' his flint axe heads by means of a process of trial, observation and adaptation. Similarly, although on a much more sophisticated level, the printing and publishing industries of the early nineteenth century depended to a great extent upon the application of rule-of-thumb procedures, whether at the compositor's bench, the engraver's table, or at the printing press. It was very rare that one man would conceive, draw up and prescribe the total form of a piece of printing in advance of production, and this is the way in which we now think of the role of the graphic designer.

The point is clearly illustrated in relation to the production of pictorial imagery. Until the late nineteenth century the drawings of the illustrative draughtsman were normally passed on to a skilled craftsman, who produced the printing surface, whether it was an engraved or etched metal plate, an engraved wood block, or a prepared lithographic stone. The craftsman-engraver had his own procedures, skills and ideals, which often completely transformed the appearance of the original drawing; nor did this transformation necessarily represent a deterioration, for draughtsmen were sometimes dependent upon their engravers to provide a degree of detail and coherence which was lacking in the original image. When the printing surface left the hands of the engraver it might well be further transformed by stages of the printing process, and the final appearance was not so much the result of one man's foresight, talent and application, as that of a chain of individuals who all contributed their part in the creation of the final product.

This brings me to the second reason why the expression 'graphic design' must be complemented by the more comprehensive 'graphic communication' in order to provide an adequate description of the content of the present book. The former term implies a stance which takes for granted the available technology of production and use: although a good contemporary graphic designer will take the technical possibilities and exploit them to the utmost, he does not normally feel responsible for making innovations in the physical techniques of production, but thinks of these as the province of the technologist in specialised fields such as type-founding, the manufacture of printing machinery, paper and ink, and, in recent years, the expanding technology of photocomposition. The contemporary graphic designer feels he is doing his duty if he can maintain as much as an intelligent understanding of the many and complex technical innovations which have characterised printing and publishing in recent years.

The technology of the nineteenth century was relatively more primitive, and there was much more overlapping of responsibilities. Printers had to know how to assemble their presses—not an easy task when it was a model they had never seen before. They had to find ways of adapting existing types to new uses, for example by mutilating one character to make another not normally available. They experimented to improve upon the poor quality of much printing ink. They struggled to cope with the exponential rise in the quantitative demand for printed matter, which required ever-faster speeds of production and created unprecedented wear in printing surfaces. In contrast to today's printing and publishing industries, those of the nineteenth century were widely dispersed outside of London. The provincial printer who encountered a technical problem could not simply pick up a telephone and confer with an expert in another town: there was no telephone; and even if there were it is quite conceivable that the problem in question had not been adequately solved by anyone, anywhere.

One must of course be careful not to exaggerate this situation. The printing industry did produce quite early a hierarchy of roles which were reasonably clearly defined in terms of their respective responsibilities in the production process; and it was recognised that certain techniques were sufficiently complex to justify the training of specialised operatives. In spite of this, the literature of the period vividly reminds one of the sense of encountering and overcoming technical problems and coping with the constantly changing circumstances of production and use. There have been few technical innovations in the twentieth century to compare with the impact of the invention of lithography, the introduction of powered printing machinery, the invention of photography, and the development of photomechanical processes, to name only a few examples, and this adds an element of adventure and excitement to the literature of the nineteenth century which is often absent in that of the twentieth.

In this welter of invention, innovation, adaptation and experiment, there was rarely if ever one controlling hand or intellect, one 'graphic designer' at the centre, attempting to prescribe for everyone in the chain of production the form of the final article. Design was a collective rather than an individual process. The rise of the graphic designer may be compared with the rise of the orchestral conductor, who by degrees forsook his place at the keyboard and his level with the rest of the orchestra, to acquire a level which was literally and metaphorically above the means of production—the orchestra—and a baton which was both the tool of his trade and an insignia of his office and authority. This simile is valid in another sense, in that the nineteenth-century orchestral musician, like the nineteenth-century printer, found himself grappling with technical problems with his instrument and with the new music of the period which nowadays, at least for the professional musician, are completely overcome.

Projects to write and publish a manual for the printer pre-date the nineteenth century, the first attempt to produce a comprehensive manual of the art of printing being Joseph Moxon *Mechanik Exercises on the Whole Art of Printing,** which appeared in twenty-four parts between 1683 and 1684. Moxon (1627-91) was a man of many talents and considerable experience, involved in several professions and pursuits other than printing, such as the making of maps and globes, hydrography, and the manufacture of mathematical instruments. His work on printing was intended to be part of a much more ambitious project covering a comprehensive range of trades and professions. It remained the most exhaustive book on the subject for more than a century after the author's death and has been re-issued several times, most recently in a version of 1962. John Smith *The Printer's Grammar* (1755) was, like Moxon's work, published in parts, and it drew heavily upon the earlier publication. Smith's *Grammar* deals only with type and composition, but it is possible that a further section on presswork was intended. Subsequent expanded editions also benefited from Moxon's pioneer work, as

*Unless otherwise stated, all books cited in the Introduction were published in London.

indeed did many later publications on printing and publishing. Stower *The Printer's Grammar* (1808)† is one such work, as well as an important document of printing in the first decade of the nineteenth century. Caleb Stower (d.1816) was a master printer active in Hackney, East London, at that time a small village some way from the city. His manual provides a great deal of information about the life and problems of the contemporary printer, including much technical information about presses and techniques. It concludes with a section of type specimens which illustrates the adoption of 'modern' continental faces with their pronounced contrasts of thick and thin as well as early display and ornamental faces, later to be much enlarged for use on handbills and posters. *Practical Hints on Decorative Printing* (1822) by William Savage (1770-1843) continued this tradition of printing manuals.

John Johnson *Typographia, or the Printer's Instructor* (1824)† appeared in several editions and different sizes. The first volume was a historical review of the history of printing largely derived from earlier authors, but Volume Two provides a valuable account of printing practice in his day, including what was then the most up-to-date description of presses and production techniques. John Johnson (1777-1848) had a varied and interesting career, setting up a press in collaboration with a wealthy country aristocrat in 1813 and later moving to London. He provides us with a great deal of information about the construction and use of hand presses, but was opposed to some of the most important technical innovations, including the use of powered printing machines and stereotyping.

Thomas Curson Hansard (1776-1833), perhaps best known for his initiation of the publication of parliamentary debates, published his *Typographia, an Historical Sketch of the Origin and Progress of the Art of Printing* in 1825.† Hansard's career illustrates one of the occupational hazards of the printer, for

C. Stower *The printer's grammar; or, introduction to the art of printing*
1808. Title page and frontispiece, 19.5 x 25 cm.

96.

THE

PRINTER'S GRAMMAR;

OR,

INTRODUCTION

TO THE

ART OF PRINTING:

CONTAINING

A CONCISE HISTORY OF THE ART,

WITH THE

IMPROVEMENTS IN THE PRACTICE OF PRINTING, FOR THE
LAST FIFTY YEARS.

BY C. STOWER, PRINTER.

Aided by thee—O Art sublime! our race
Spurns the opposing bonds of time and space,
With Fame's swift flight to hold an equal course,
And taste the stream from Reason's purest source;
Vice and her hydra sons, thy powers can bind,
And cast in Virtue's mould the plastic mind.
M'Creery.

LONDON:

Printed by the Editor, 32, Paternoster Row,

FOR B. CROSBY AND CO. STATIONERS'-COURT.

1808.

John Johnson *Typographia, or the printers' instructor* 1824,
Vol. 2. Title page and portrait of Johnson, 14 x 17.5 cm.

T. C. Hansard *Typographia* 1825. Title page and frontispiece,
22.8 x 27.6 cm.

TYPOGRAPHIA:

AN HISTORICAL SKETCH

OF

THE ORIGIN AND PROGRESS OF

THE ART OF PRINTING;

WITH

PRACTICAL DIRECTIONS FOR CONDUCTING EVERY DEPARTMENT IN AN OFFICE:

WITH A DESCRIPTION OF

STEREOTYPE AND LITHOGRAPHY.

ILLUSTRATED BY

Engravings, Biographical Notices, and Portraits.

BY T. C. HANSARD.

PRINTED FOR

BALDWIN, CRADOCK, AND JOY: LONDON.

1825.

in 1810 he was imprisoned as a result of his publication of a libel dealing with military flogging. His *Typographia* covered every aspect of the printer's work, including the techniques of stereotyping and lithography. In 1841 he published a *Treatise on Printing*. He is not to be confused with his son Thomas Curson Hansard the barrister, who also wrote several books on the history of printing.

Timperley *The Printer's Manual* (1838)† provides much evidence of the state of the industry during the opening years of the Victorian era. Charles H Timperley (1794-1846?) had a colourful career, beginning as a copperplate engraver in Manchester and later becoming a letterpress printer, editor and author in the Midlands. He enlisted in the army in 1810 and was discharged after being wounded at Waterloo. Timperley was also a poet, compiling and writing an important collection of printer's songs and poetry entitled *Songs of the Press and other Poems* (1833). Timperley wrote at a time when printing and publishing had been overtaken by an unprecedented demand for increased quantity and speed of production, and much of his manual deals with innovations such as the all-metal presses which were designed to cope with the increased pressures and speed of production. As he himself put it, 'the old wooden press is nearly exploded'. However, his emphasis on manual presses and physical labour is evidence of the continuing importance of short-run work in the jobbing printing of his day, the most important innovations in machine presses having taken place in newspaper and periodical publication.

There are many technical manuals which deal with selected aspects of printing and publishing, such as La Lande *L'Art de faire papier* (Paris, c.1750) and J. Murray *Practical Remarks on Modern Paper* (Edinburgh, 1829). One of the most intractable problems of the nineteenth century printer was to find inks which satisfied all the technical and aesthetic requirements of different jobs, which would print easily, dry quickly (an essential feature of newspaper and periodical printing), look good, and would not fade or spread ugly stains as a result of the oil content. William Savage *On the Preparation of Printing Ink; Both Black and Coloured* (1832)† is the most important publication of its period on the subject. William Savage (1770-1843), the son of a Yorkshire clock-maker, commenced business as a printer in the North of England before moving to London in 1797 to become the official printer to the Royal Institution. He later expanded into business on his own account, undertaking work on such prestigious publications as Forster's *British Gallery of Engravings* and at the same time becoming involved with experiments on improved inks. Between 1822 and 1832 he was busy compiling a *Dictionary of the Art of Printing*†, which appeared in 1841, when it was at once recognised as a work of great authority. In his dictionary, Savage gives us a useful outline of the career profile of the successful printer of his day, rising from apprentice to compositor and, if he proved to be a capable workman, to reader, overseer, and perhaps opening a business of his own and employing others. Savage had a typically Victorian attitude to the question of the interdependence of good work and good morals, combined with a taste for the niceties of composition and spacing which was lamentably absent in much of the printing of his day and in the decades to follow.

An important complement to technical manuals is provided by the numerous books of type specimens published by type founders and distributors in increasing quantities after about 1800 in response to the rapid growth of the industry and the demand for typographic variety. One of the foremost of these is the series put out by the firm of Vincent Figgins (1776-1844), who set up as an independent founder in London about 1792 and published numerous books of type specimens advertising his wares. Figgins was responsible for promoting many of the innovations in type design, such as the popularisation of egyptian, shadowed and sanserif faces.

All the publications so far mentioned appeared as a result

of private enterprise by printers, publishers and authors, but this source of material is complemented by a growing output of official documents published by the state and its agencies. Governments, local and national administrations increasingly recognized printing as an essential key to effective government, education and political propaganda, and many official publications reflect this concern to control and utilise printing in what were seen as the interests of the state. The *Report* of the Parliamentary Select Committee on Art and Manufactures (1836) illustrates this trend in connection with the need to use printing and what was called 'the paper circulation of knowledge' as a means of improving British industry and design.

Official documents such as the *Public Libraries Act* of 1850 represent milestones in the campaign to extend the influence of education and literacy to the whole population, a process which was regarded as essential to the healthy evolution of the state in the post-industrial era. Another aspect of public and official involvement is to be found in the organisation of national and international exhibitions and trade fairs, commencing with the Great Exhibition of 1851 held in London. *The Official Descriptive and Illustrated Catalogue* contained, like many subsequent exhibition reports, the most up-to-date accounts of printing techniques of the day and serves as a useful reference work.

The central concern of many of the manuals of the early nineteenth century was the printing and publishing of texts in letterpress, by which is meant printing from movable types in relief. An essential complement to this area of the industry was the development of techniques for the production of pictorial imagery in the form of illustrations for books, periodicals and ephemera, as well as independent prints for collectors and for exhibition in the home and in galleries. The tradition of technical manuals dealing with the preparation and printing of pictorial imagery goes back to Abraham Bosse *Traicté des manières de graver en taille-douce* (Paris,

1645), which covers the variety of methods of printing in intaglio, a term which means that the image to be printed is incised into a metal plate.

Intaglio printing, which is capable of great refinement and variety of effect, was given a special boost by the growing taste for illustrated magazines that was a feature of the late eighteenth century. Many of these, like *The Artist's Repository and Drawing Magazine* (1785-1795), were of an artistic nature, including illustrated articles on art, design, fashion and travel. Rudolph Ackermann (1764-1834) was, more than any other single person, responsible for promoting and satisfying the taste for fine printed imagery. He was born and educated in Saxony, but moved to England and in 1795 married an English woman and opened his famous print shop in The Strand, London. His numerous activities included publishing and writing, and he even ran a drawing school for a period until his other pursuits absorbed the whole of his time and energy. Ackermann's principal achievement was the publication of the periodical known as *Repository of Arts, Literature, Commerce, etc.*, which appeared between 1809 and 1828 and set unprecedented standards of quality in its numerous illustrations of art works, furniture and contemporary costume. He also played a central role in the introduction of lithography into Britain.

The intaglio processes may be divided into two families of techniques, namely those like line-engraving, in which the image is incised by a sharp tool under the pressure of the engraver's hand, and those, like etching and aquatint, in which the image is bitten into the plate by immersion in an acid solution. There are of course numerous variations on these basic techniques, such as drypoint, aquatint and mezzotint. Very high cultural and aesthetic prestige was attached to line engraving, mainly, in the days before photography, as a means of reproducing art works. Skilled reproductive engravers were in high demand and were paid enormous sums of money for engraving plates which were calculated to reap large profits for the publisher by satisfying the public demand for high quality illustrations and parlour prints. Publications like C. F. Partingon *The Engraver's Complete Guide* (1825) and Berthiau and Boitard *Nouveau manuel complet de l'imprimeur en taille-douce* (Paris, 1836) exemplify the intense interest in intaglio printing, as does much evidence which appeared in official reports and documents, such as John Pye *Evidence Relating to the Art of Engraving Taken before the Select Committee of the House of Commons on the Arts* (1836).

Many of the most prominent engravers had a background or a continuing parallel practice in some aspect of the fine arts, writing or publishing. Theodore Henry Fielding (1781-1851) was a prolific painter and author as well as a versatile master of engraving, etching, stipple and aquatint. Of his numerous publications, the most interesting one in the present context is *The Art of Engraving* (1841)† which provides much essential information about the practices and tastes current in his day. However, the principal role of the intaglio processes in the pre-photographic era was not the production of original prints, but the reproduction of existing works such as paintings, sculpture, architecture and ornamental design. Its role as a reproductive medium was rapidly undermined by the advent of photography and, more importantly, photo-mechanical reproduction, and by the second half of the century most intaglio printing was confined to two areas of activity, the printing of work with special requirements, such as bank notes, and the revived field of autographic etching. However, a continuing interest in and respect for the conventions of reproductive engraving is evident as late as the last quarter of the century, in works such as Henri Delaborde *La gravure* (Paris, c.1885).

The printing of pictorial material was revolutionised by the invention of lithography by Senefelder in 1796-8. Aloysius (or Alois) Senefelder (1771-1834) of Munich had experimented for some time in the quest for a cheap and efficient means of printing texts and music. His early experiments were based on the notion of creating an image etched in low relief on stone, but this approach was superseded by one which simply exploited the incompatibility of grease and water. An image was drawn with a greasy crayon on fine-grained limestone. The surface of the stone was dampened and then rolled with a roller charged with a grease-based ink. The drawn image, which repelled the water, accepted the ink from the roller, while the undrawn areas of the stone, which had absorbed the water into its pores, rejected the ink. Following this simple principle, it was possible to re-charge and print the image many times. The great advantage of lithography was that unlike media such as line engraving or wood engraving it required no special skills for the creation of the printing surface, other than the ability to draw: drawing on a lithographic stone was almost identical to drawing on paper, and at a very early stage a technique was evolved for drawing the image on prepared paper and then transferring it on to stone. Lithography opened the way to a splendid tradition of graphic art of immense variety and quality, including autographic prints by artists of considerable reputation, such as Goya, Delacroix and Manet.

Lithography had two principal disadvantages. The first was that its technical procedures were inherently different from those of letterpress and other relief media. Lithographs had to be printed on special presses by operatives with special skills; consequently any publication which combined lithography with, for example, letterpress text had to draw its contents from two quite disparate sources. Secondly, because of the novelty of the medium and peculiar problems attendant on the printing process its spread was inhibited by the dearth of reliable technical information. The first problem was partly overcome by printing some work entirely by lithography, including text and pictorial material. The technical distinctions between lithography and letterpress meant, however, that it could never rival wood engraving in quantity as a source of periodical and book illustration. The second problem, that of the availability of technical information and know-how, was gradually overcome by the publication and circulation of manuals and instructional books. Works about lithography and specimens of lithographic printing began to appear soon after its invention, such as the 1803 publication *Specimens of Polyautography* (one of several names applied to lithography in its infancy). Senefelder was so preoccupied with developing and perfecting his invention that he did not publish his own manual until 1818, entitled *Vollständiges Lehrbuch der Steindruckerey* (Munich and Vienna, 1818). This appeared in English as *A Complete Course of Lithography* (1819)† and was published in London by Ackermann.

Charles Joseph Hullmandel (1789-1850), the son of a German musician living in London, was attracted to lithography as a way of multiplying drawings done on his foreign travels. After a short and unsatisfactory period of studying the medium with a lithographic firm in Paris he left to pursue the subject on his own account, and in 1824 published the most important work in English to appear in the first half of the nineteenth century, entitled *The Art of Drawing on Stone*. Hullmandel's book, like G. Engelmann *Manuel du dessinateur lithographe* (Paris, 1822) was concerned with the techniques and styles of drawing on the stone, rather than with the problems of printing, and it played a crucial role in educating draughtsmen for the exploitation of the possibilities of the medium.

In spite of its considerable expressive potential, the status of lithography was somewhat prejudiced by its widespread employment in commecial printing and advertising, as well as by the production of tasteless chromolithographs of unspeakable quality. Several prominent authors of the last quarter of the century felt the need to aid the revival of lithography as a respected autographic medium by exonerating it from its tradition of commercial exploitation. As late as 1894 William Rothenstein, himself an eminent graphic

A COMPLETE

COURSE OF LITHOGRAPHY:

CONTAINING

Clear and Explicit Instructions

IN ALL THE

DIFFERENT BRANCHES AND MANNERS OF THAT ART:

ACCOMPANIED BY

ILLUSTRATIVE SPECIMENS OF DRAWINGS.

TO WHICH IS PREFIXED A

HISTORY OF LITHOGRAPHY,

FROM ITS ORIGIN TO THE PRESENT TIME.

By ALOIS SENEFELDER,

INVENTOR OF THE ART OF LITHOGRAPHY AND CHEMICAL PRINTING.

WITH

A PREFACE

By FREDERIC VON SCHLICHTEGROLL,

Director of the Royal Academy of Sciences at Munich.

TRANSLATED FROM THE ORIGINAL GERMAN, BY A. S.

London:

PRINTED FOR R. ACKERMANN, 101, STRAND.

1819.

Alois Senefelder *A complete course of lithography* 1819.
Title page, 27 x 20.5 cm.

artist, wrote: 'It is a strange thing that, of late years, lithography should, with but few exceptions, have chiefly been confined to the production of fashion-plates and grocers' almanacks . . . This art, answering—though not perhaps at first—so exquisitely to the touch of its constant lover, has been even as a galley-slave in the hands of a base commercialism, and so besmirched that but few could recognise its true fairness.' (*The Studio*, Vol. III, p.16.)

For several reasons, including those already indicated, neither the intaglio processes nor lithography were capable of satisfying the rapidly rising demand for illustrative material. What was needed was a method of printing pictures which was compatible with letterpress in the sense of being capable of production on the same presses, if necessary in the same forme, as the related text. This need was supplied by the development of the wood engraving. Until the opening of the last quarter of the eighteenth century printing from wood had occupied a relatively lowly status in comparison with its leading rival, line engraving, and its use was confined mainly to the production of decorative borders and rather crude illustrations for books and broadsheets. J.M. Papillon *Traité historique et pratique de la gravure en bois* (Paris, 1776), an important document of its day, predates the revival of printing from wood.

This revival was initiated and sustained by the Northumberland engraver and draughtsman, Thomas Bewick (1753-1828). Inspired by his love of nature and art, Bewick applied his ingenuity to the development of improved engraving tools and techniques. While the older woodcut was produced on the side (or plank) grain of soft wood, and was only capable of relatively crude imagery, the wood engraving was made on the end grain of a hard wood, chiefly box, and was capable of immense detail and subtlety. Although difficult to describe in words, the principle of Bewick's technique was that rather than simply clearing the 'white' areas away from the drawn image to leave lines standing up in black, he employed the graver as a positive drawing tool, progressively introducing white into the back of the block to create a rich variety of forms, tones and textures. In this way, he 'drew' with the graver, rather than simply apeing the work of the draughts-man, whether it was himself or someone else. This 'white line' technique of wood engraving was used in a series of works which he illustrated during the closing years of the eighteenth century, notably his *General History of Quad-rupeds*, which was begun in 1785 and the *History of British Birds*, the first volume of which appeared in 1797.

A pupil of Bewick, John Jackson (1801-48) became the first wood engraver to work for popular literature and jour-nalism, and he played an important role in the development of Charles Knight's *Penny Magazine*. During Jackson's life-time, wood engraving expanded from a minor trade to a veritable industry, making an essential contribution to the enormously increased and diversified world of publishing in the Victorian era. Jackson was keenly interested in the origins and history of his profession and for some years collected information and specimens of the art of wood engraving. He teamed up with a close friend, the author and journalist William Andrew Chatto (1799-1864), and in 1839 they produced the first edition of *A Treatise on Wood Engraving*†, undoubtedly the most comprehensive book ever published on the subject. Jackson originated the project, provided the capital, wrote much of the content and did many of the engravings (which included much of his best work), while Chatto contributed his literary and editing skills. The result is an indispensable work for the student of wood engraving. The authors cover every aspect of the subject, ranging from drawing and cutting techniques to occupational diseases, notably short sight which resulted from long periods of fine work combined with repeated re-focusing of the eyes. The authors' friendship was subse-quently terminated by a bitter dispute as to their relative contributions to the work and they parted sworn enemies.

A second expanded edition of the *Treatise* was published in 1861.

Several wood engravers tried their hand at writing a manual, a good example being Thomas Gilks *The Art of Wood-Engraving. A Practical Handbook* (1866)†. Gilks takes a rather simple-minded approach to the subject, concentrating on the tricks of the trade such as the depiction of volumes in light and shade and the rendering of different textures. William James Linton (1812-1898), in his *Wood-Engraving. A Manual of Instruction* (1884)†, was capable of seeing the medium in a social and historical perspective, and expressed his distaste for many of the consequences of the vastly increased output of illustrated work. Linton deplored brainless facsimile engraving as much as he hated what he regarded as gimmicky 'impressionist' work which was intended to capture every nuance of a painted original. His ideal was a style of white line work based upon the example of Bewick and his school. In 1866 Linton went to the USA and there published *The Masters of Wood-Engraving* (New Haven, 1889), a celebration, and at the same time the swan-song, of the whole art of wood engraving; for by this time the medium was being rapidly overtaken by the cheaper and faster methods of photomechanical reproduction. Assessments and retrospects of the art of wood engraving continued to appear up to the end of the century and beyond, such as F. Bracquemond *Etude sur la gravure sur bois et la lithographie* (Paris, 1897), and G. and E. Dalziel *The Brothers Dalziel. A Record of Work 1840-1890* (1901), which provides a history of one of the most important wood engraving firms in the world. This can be amplified by study of the many periodicals and books which were illustrated with wood engravings, such as *Punch* 1841-) and *The Illustrated London News* (1842-).

M. H. Spielmann *The History of Punch* (1895) provides a thorough, if inevitably partisan, review of the history of that magazine during its first half-century. A more comprehensive study of illustrated journalism in the mid-nineteenth century is to be found in Mason Jackson *The Pictorial Press: Its Origins and Progress* (1884)†. Mason Jackson (1819-1903) was the younger brother of John Jackson (mentioned above), who gave him his first lessons in wood engraving. He showed great talent and aptitude, and made an outstanding reputation as a prolific illustrator of a variety of publications, including the magazines *Art Union* and *Illustrated London News*. He held the position of art editor of the latter for some thirty years. Mason Jackson, like his brother John, had an intense interest in the history of his profession, and his book is rich with information, comment and anecdote, providing a vivid picture of publishing during his lifetime. Many of the technical procedures which he describes arose in response to the increased pressures and speeds of presses and production in the mid-nineteenth century. These include the practice of dividing large blocks into sections so that they could be engraved simultaneously by several engravers and then re-assembled before printing. By this time, printing was usually done from stereotypes (duplicate casts of the original block) rather than from the wooden block itself; periodical publishers could not risk the consequences of a split block in the middle of a print run. During the 1870s the wood engraving industry was more or less obliterated by photomechanical techniques, and it survived only as a minority autographic technique used for the illustration of books produced by the private presses. The magazine *L'Image*, which was launched by the French Association of Wood Engravers and was dedicated to a revival of the art, was founded in 1896 and closed in 1897.

The rate of technical innovation during the nineteenth century meant that printers and publishers often found themselves working at the limits of the state of the art as it existed; indeed, these limits were frequently transgressed—with disastrous consequences in terms of technical breakdowns and ruined print runs. No doubt many jobbing printers in small provincial towns were able to maintain their livelihood

L'Image No. 12, December 1897. Cover, 29.8 x 21.5 cm.

with the techniques and methods which they had learned as apprentices, but the whole business of publishing and printing was changing so fast that the larger book and periodical publishers could not afford to be complacent: failure to grasp the significance and the advantages of new technology often led to economic ruin in the face of competitors who succeeded in doing so. For example, firms of wood engravers who diversified at the right time into photomechanical work survived; those who stuck rigidly to wood engraving soon found themselves without a livelihood.

In this kind of climate it was inevitable that the whole process of invention and the improvement of inventions became one of intense interest. A valuable source of insight into the introduction of new inventions is provided by patent specifications, which present verbal and diagrammatic information about the devices in question. These are available at the London Patent Office, as indeed they are at comparable institutions in other countries. Of special interest in relation to the history of graphic communication are the abridgements of printing patents published by the Patent Office. The first of these appeared in 1859 and was entitled *Patents for Inventions. Abridgements of Specifications relating to Printing* (etc.).

Inventors, who were often themselves printers, attempted to protect their inventions by obtaining a grant of patent, which gave them a monopoly over their device for a specified period of time. The grant of a patent enables an inventor to prevent competitors from using the same device, even if they hit upon the idea subsequently and without knowledge of the existing patent. Alternatively, the inventor could licence others to use the device upon the payment of an appropriate fee. However, patent specifications do not provide a complete guide to new inventions, since inventors often had good reasons for not patenting a device. The grant of a patent normally requires disclosure of the invention in the form of drawings and descriptions. This may lead to illicit copying, which, if detected, can only be prevented by expensive legal action; or, even worse, a competitor might develop an invention which exploits the principles of the original device but incorporates features which place it outside of the patent specification. Moreover, when the patent has elapsed the invention moves into the public domain, and may be copied by anyone with impunity.

For these and other reasons many inventions in printing, as in other spheres of production, were never patented but kept as trade secrets known to only one or a small number of employees—for the same reason that the formula for Coca Cola has never been disclosed but is known by only a tiny number of the company's employees. It was claimed that in some photomechanical engravers' workshops even the estimator for insurance was not allowed to see the equipment, which was kept covered with sheets during his visit, with the consequence that it could never be insured.

Occasionally whole books or reports were devoted to specialised technical problems, such as J. H. Ibbetson *A Practical View of an Invention for Better Protecting Bank-Notes Against Forgery* (1821). Thomas Spencer *Instructions for the Multiplication of Works of Art in Metal by Voltaic Electricity* (Glasgow, 1840) heralded one of the most important inventions of the day, namely a method of using electrolytic deposition as a means of creating facsimiles of printing surfaces. This was a vital factor not only in preserving wooden blocks from excessive wear or destruction, but in enabling the printer to produce a large print run of a periodical or newspaper quickly by printing on more than one machine simultaneously. The importance of both stereotyping and electrotyping is further discussed in F. H. F. Wilson *Stereotyping and Electrotyping* (1880).

More general conspectuses of the techniques of the graphic arts are given in C. Tomlinson *Cyclopaedia of Useful Arts* (1854) and John Donlevy's brief but interesting survey *The Rise and Progress of the Graphic Arts* (New York, 1854). A valuable and extremely rare source which provides descriptions of numerous printing techniques together with examples is W. J. Stannard *The Art Exemplar* (c.1859), published in an edition of only ten copies. Many of the 156 processes listed by Stannard have now fallen into obscurity, but a knowledge of their existence is useful in forming a picture of printing and publishing in his day.

As well as being a kind of manufacturing industry in its own right, printing and publishing played an important secondary role as virtually the sole medium for advertising, a role which it now shares with radio, television and film. William Smith, manager of the New Adelphi Theatre in London published *Advertise. How? When? Where?* in 1863†. His book provides a rich and amusing account of the role and character of advertising in his day, together with some suggestions for improvements and even a crude attempt at a statistical survey, based on empirical observation. The rise of interest in the function of advertising is continued in H. Sampson *A History of Advertising from the Earliest Times* (1874). These works represent the beginnings of the interest in the scientific study of advertising which continues in some twentieth-century publications, such as H. E. Burtt *The Psychology of Advertising* (Boston, 1938)†.

One of the consequences of the industrial revolution was the generation of unprecedented quantities of printed matter. The processes of the manufacture and circulation of goods on a massive scale required the production of all kinds of documents, such as advertising matter, bills, invoices, receipts, statements of account and of course bank notes, the number of which in circulation increased rapidly during the nineteenth century. A high proportion of workers in the manufacturing and service industries were now required to read and write; this led to ambitious national schemes for public education, commencing in Britain in the 1830s. Soon a majority of the public was literate, and the ability to read created a second wave of demand for printed matter which was not essential to the wheels of industry, but provided entertainment and a leisure occupation, such as popular magazines, novels, books of poetry and cheap prints.

A proportion of this vastly increased volume of production was of remarkable quality in both technical and aesthetic terms; but inevitably the demand for quantity combined with cheapness and the existence of an avid and rather undiscriminating public encouraged the production of a great deal of printed matter which was either dull and mechanical in character or in thoroughly bad taste. The second half of the nineteenth century is characterised by the appearance of articulate prophets of doom like John Ruskin and William Morris who were highly critical of the direction which the whole of industrial output—including the manufacture of printed matter—had taken.

Perhaps this was one contributory factor to the vigorous revival of interest in autographic prints which took place during the last thirty years of the century; for the ability to show discrimination in the selection and evaluation of printed matter was a hallmark of the connoisseur, and something which set him apart from the general public. There were probably other reasons. The revival flourished in France and is perhaps not unrelated to the fact that in the 1870s as a result of the disastrous Franco-Prussian war there was a catastrophic slump in the French economy. The economic crisis led to a collapse of public commissions as a source of livelihood for artists, who were forced to turn to the production of works which were modest in scale and could be sold at a low unit price. In painting this heralded the generally small canvases of the Impressionists (1874-) and also a revival of interest in autographic prints.

Several authors turned their attention to graphic art and graphic communication, including of course Ruskin himself who had very decided opinions on the subject. One of the most prolific and capable of these authors was Philip Gilbert Hamerton (1834-1894), whose numerous publications played an important role in shaping the tastes of the new public for fine prints. Hamerton at first cultivated the twin ambitions of becoming a painter and an author, and it is perhaps fortunate for us that he abandoned painting to concentrate his time and energies on writing, although he did continue to produce etchings of a rather amateurish quality. After a series of minor publications of poetry and criticism, Hamerton was commissioned to write a work on etching, and this appeared as *Etching and Etchers* in 1868. Shortly after this he was involved in a scheme to produce a quality periodical on the graphic arts, which commenced publication in 1870 as *The Portfolio*. *The Portfolio* (1870-1893) was illustrated with etchings, autotypes, Woodburytypes and photogravure, and both its text and illustrations provided a significant source of interest and stimulus for the growing revival in autographic prints. Hamerton's publications are too numerous to mention in detail here, but one of the most important is *The Graphic Arts* (1882)†, which not only presents a useful conspectus of the state of the graphic arts in his day, but contains some of the most perceptive writing about the nature of graphic imagery which I believe has ever been published. He continued to write and publish up until the time of his death, *Drawing and Engraving* appearing in 1892, as well as contributing prints to many exhibitions and publications.

The Portfolio was only one of a growing volume of illustrated magazines about art, such as the *Illustrated Magazine of Art* (1853-   ), *Die graphischen Künste* (1879-) and *English Etchings* (1881-91). Many of these were illustrated with wood engravings, perhaps supported by the insertion of an etching as a frontispiece, and not all of them were of any great quality as specimens of graphic art.

The revival of etching was punctuated by a series of publications dealing with the history of the medium, technical procedures and aesthetic evaluation. Maxime Lalanne *A Treatise on Etching* appeared in French in 1866 and in English in 1880†. One of the most important English etchers was

THE GRAPHIC ARTS

A TREATISE ON THE VARIETIES OF DRAWING, PAINTING, AND ENGRAVING

IN COMPARISON WITH EACH OTHER

AND WITH NATURE

BY

PHILIP GILBERT HAMERTON

AUTHOR OF 'ETCHING AND ETCHERS'

ETC. ETC. ETC.

'There is a great advantage in thorough technical training which must not be over-looked. When a man learns anything thoroughly it teaches him to respect what he learns. It teaches him to delight in his task for its own sake, and not for the sake of pay or reward. The happiness of our lives depends less on the actual value of the work which we do than on the spirit in which we do it. If a man tries to do the simplest and humblest work as well as he possibly can, he will be interested in it; he will be proud of it. But if, on the other hand, he only thinks of what he can get by his work, then the highest work will soon become wearisome.'

Prince Leopold's Speech at Nottingham, June 30th, 1881.

LONDON

SEELEY, JACKSON, AND HALLIDAY, FLEET STREET

1882

P. G. Hamerton *The graphic arts* 1882. Title page, 29.5 x 20.5 cm.

Whistler's brother-in-law, the surgeon Francis Seymour Haden (1818-1910). Haden studied surgery in London, then studied and worked in Paris and Grenoble. During his period in France he was employed as a surgeon during the day and attended art school during the evening. There can be little doubt that his publications, as well as his numerous etchings, played a significant role in developing and forming the taste for etchings in Britain. One of Haden's major contributions to the literature and criticism of art was his intensive study and evaluation of Rembrandt's graphic work. His *About Etching* (1879), first prepared as an essay for the catalogue of an exhibition of etchings, helps us to understand the tastes and enthusiasms which motivated the protagonists of the etching revival. Works on etching continued to appear frequently up to the end of the century and beyond, including F. Short *On the Making of Etchings* (1888), F. Wedmore *Etchings in England* (1895) and H. Paton *Etching, Drypoint, Mezzotint. The Whole Art of the Painter-Etcher. A Practical Treatise* (1895). Although etching tends to be the medium most closely associated with the revival of autographic printmaking, several other media played significant roles, including lithography. This too led to parallel publications such as W. D. Richmond *The Grammar of Lithography* (1878). The boom in autographic prints carried over to the first two decades of the twentieth century before going into an economic decline at the time of the great Depression of the 1920s. A reference work which provides a guide to the period of the revival is H. C. Levis *A Descriptive Bibliography of the Most Important Books in the English Language Relating to the Art and History of Engraving and the Collecting of Prints* (1912-13).

It has already been necessary to mention photography and photo-mechanical reproduction and their influence on the printing of imagery. Photography was invented during the late 1820s, but it was some considerable time before it had any significant effect on graphic communication and printing.

Early photographs were slow and expensive to produce; their permanence was, quite justifiably, suspect; and although they had a recognised role in reportage there was no obvious way in which they could serve as a substitute for graphic imagery which expressed visions of the imagination, fictions, projects and intentions. P. G. Hamerton summed up this problem perfectly when he wrote: 'But there is one fatal objection to photography in comparison with drawing, an objection which far outweighs all the others, and that is, the necessity for an actually existing model. You cannot photograph an intention, whilst you *can* draw an intention, even in the minutest detail . . .' (*The Graphic Arts*, 1882, p.9). There was a short-lived attempt to use real photographic prints as illustrations in books which reached a peak in the 1860s, but, quite apart from the enormous expense of producing photographs in the number required and having to stick them into the work, their unsuitability for fiction was self-evident. The sight of conspicuously Victorian ladies dressed in muslin robes, holding statuesque poses and surrounded by theatrical props in an attempt to recreate some scene from medieval literature is unlikely to evoke any response other than amusement.

What was needed was not so much the use of photographs *per se*, but the exploitation of photographic processes in conjunction with existing printing techniques. This possibility began to emerge in the 1860s, when a technique was discovered for transferring a photograph on to a wood engraver's block. This could be used to transfer either photographs of original drawings, or actual photographs taken from nature, although it was still necessary for the wood engraver to interpret the image in his own way.

The next step, which came soon afterwards, was the ability to photograph a line drawing and transfer it completely automatically—without any intervention of the manual engraver—on to a metal printing surface. This technique was perfected very rapidly during the 1870s, leading to the creation of photomechanical reproduction proper, often referred to in nineteenth-century sources as 'photomechanical process' or simply 'process'. Although in quantitative terms the most important method of photomechanical reproduction was done from metal relief blocks, the technique was also applied to intaglio processes and to lithography; indeed, it is the last-named technique, in the form of photolithography, which has come to dominate the printing of the present day. The development of photomechanical line reproduction was soon to be complemented by methods for interpreting continuous gradations of tone in the creation of printing surfaces. The invention of the so-called 'half-tone' process enabled the printer to reproduce works such as wash drawings and of course original photographs.

The literature surrounding the emergence of photomechanical processes is rather fragmentary up until the 1880s, one of the most important accounts appearing in E. Y. Grupe *Instructions in the Art of Photographing on Wood* (Leominster, Massachusetts, 1882). From this date onwards there appeared a stream of publications on every aspect of the subject, notably J. S. Hodson *An Historical and Practical Guide to Art Illustration* (1884), W. K. Burton *Practical Guide to Photographic and Photo-mechanical Printing* (1892) and Herbert Denison *Treatise on Photogravure in Intaglio by the Talbot-Klič Process* (1895)†. This period in the history of printing and publishing is described in Geoffrey Wakeman *Victorian Book Illustration* (Newton Abbot, 1973).

A common phenomenon in the history of graphic communication is that in the early days of a new technique authors and practitioners tend to be preoccupied with mastering and communicating the technical aspects of the medium. As these are overcome and taken for granted, attention switches to the aesthetic and expressive exploitation of the medium. This development is noticeable in the literature surrounding photomechanical reproduction, for with the 1890s we find a declining interest in the purely technical potential and problems of the medium, and a correspondingly greater preoccupation with methods of drawing and the exploitation of its expressive qualities. In this category we include works by practising illustrators, such as Henry Blackburn *The Art of Illustration* (1894), C. G. Harper *Practical Handbook of Drawing for Modern Methods of Reproduction* (1894)†, A. Horsley Hinton *A Handbook of Illustration* (1894) and Charles J. Vine *Hints on Drawing for Process Reproduction* (1895). Much of Harper's book had already appeared in *The Studio* as a series of articles dealing with such problems as the creation of tonal gradation in line work.

One individual deserves special mention, since he occupies in connection with photomechanical reproduction a position of importance comparable with that of Hamerton in relation to the autographic revival. This is the American illustrator and author Joseph Pennell (1857-1926). Pennell was born and educated in Philadelphia. In 1881 his drawings began to appear in magazines, at that time reproduced as wood engravings. He came to Europe in 1883 and remained for nearly thirty years, returning to the USA in 1912. During his period in Europe, spent mainly in England but with numerous excursions to the Continent, Pennell was deeply involved with the artistic life of the times, becoming a close associate of Whistler and eventually co-authoring with his able and industrious wife one of the most substantial biographies of that artist.

But Pennell will be best remembered for his championing of photomechanical reproduction, and his crusade to make the public accept line illustration, which he referred to as 'pen drawing', as an artistic form in its own right, related to but distinct from both reproductive and autographic prints. His *Pen Drawing and Pen Draughtsmen* (1889)† is an essential document of the period, and this was followed by *Modern Illustration* (1895), which strongly asserted the unique role of photomechanical reproduction in illustration. Pennell was

PEN DRAWING AND PEN DRAUGHTSMEN

THEIR WORK AND THEIR ME THODS A STUDY OF THE ART TO-DAY WITH TECH NICAL SUGGESTIONS BY JOSEPH PENNELL

LECTURER ON ILLUSTRATION AT THE
SLADE SCHOOL UNIVERSITY COLLEGE

MACMILLAN AND COMPANY
LONDON AND NEW YORK
MDCCCXCIV

Joseph Pennell *Pen drawing and pen draughtsmen* (1889) 1894.
Title page, 29 x 22 cm.

also responsible for 'discovering' the young Aubrey Beardsley, in an enthusiastic article which he wrote for the first issue of *The Studio*, April 1893. Pennell's enthusiasm for Beardsley is a testament to his discrimination and catholicity of taste, for a comparison of Beardsley's drawings with Pennell's own work will reveal that they had two completely opposed artistic sensibilities. Pennell also published several works on autographic processes, such as *Lithography and Lithographers* (1898), and these, too, provide much useful information and illuminating views on the graphic arts. From his autobiography *Adventures of an Illustrator* (1925) we can build a picture of Pennell as a talented, energetic, if rather opinionated and irascible individual; much of his published work was characteristically dictated to his wife whilst pacing up and down the drawing room. The complete *Life and Letters of Joseph Pennell* was published by his wife Elizabeth Robins Pennell in 1930.

The vast majority of printed matter, including autographic prints, was, and remains, monochromatic. Printing in colour has always posed a number of technical and economic problems, with the result that coloured matter was often prohibitively difficult or expensive. Beginning in the 1830s there was renewed interest in colour amongst both artists and scientists. The French scientist M. E. Chevreul published his influential treatise on colour in French in 1839, and this was translated and appeared in English as *The Principles of Harmony and Contrast of Colours, and their Application to the Arts* (1855). Successful printing in full colour depended upon a number of related technical breakthroughs, the most important of these being the perfection of photomechanical reproduction, the development of good quality coloured inks, and finally a method of screening colour work and breaking it down into its constituent hues, thereby enabling the production of colour separation blocks or plates.

John Earhart *The Colour Printer* (Cincinnati, 1892) is a useful account of the position at the end of the nineteenth century. A longer and more detailed study together with many specimens of work, appears in R. M. Burch *Colour Printing and the Colour Printer* (1910). Some idea of the state of colour photography during the first decade of the twentieth century can be gained from Charles Holme (ed.) *Colour Photography*, published as a supplement to *The Studio* in 1908.

Joseph Pennell was quite justifiably regarded as a progressive or radical figure in his day, although he did have an acute appreciation of the graphic art of the past. During the 1890s there appeared a contrary tendency to look to the past, celebrating, recording and reviving its finest qualities. There was a feeling that the end of an era was at hand, heralding a complete transformation of all the arts, including graphic art. Authors and artists began to look back to the heyday of wood-engraved illustration in the 1860s with a feeling of nostalgia and perhaps some regret. During his career as an author, editor, critic and designer, Gleeson White (1851-1898) assembled one of the best private libraries of illustrated books, and in 1897 published *English Illustration 'The Sixties': 1855-70*, a remarkable anthology of that period of illustration which has since been followed by several similar studies. A conservative or even reactionary tendency is evident in Walter Crane *The Decorative Illustration of Books* (1896). Although Crane (1845-1915) had been in the forefront of good illustration during the middle of his career he came to regard the influence of photomechanical reproduction with great suspicion and deplored the most characteristic drawings of Beardsley for what he felt were their lack of structure. Crane's autobiography *An Artist's Reminiscences* (1907) is, like Pennell's autobiography, a rich and informative source.

Books on the techniques and styles of illustration continued to pour forth after the turn of the century, and indeed continue today. As examples one may mention R. E. D. Sketchley *English Book Illustration of Today* (1903), T. G. Hill *The*

Essentials of Illustration (1915) and, a noteworthy book by a talented illustrator, Edmund J. Sullivan *The Art of Illustration* (1921)†. Later examples of the species include Ashley Havinden *Line Drawing for Reproduction* (1933) and Lynton Lamb *Drawing for Illustration* (1962).

The second half of the nineteenth century is marked by a steady increase in the level of professional organisation of printers. This is reflected in the foundation of numerous periodicals dealing with all aspects of the industry. The first of these, *The Printer's Register*, appeared in July 1863. It was followed by *The Printing Times* (1873), which merged in the following year with *The Lithographer* to become *The Printing Times and Lithographer*, the periodical which was responsible for publishing, between 1876 and 1885, Bigmore and Wyman's seminal *Bibliography of Printing* (see below). *The British and Colonial Printer and Stationer* was founded in 1878, changing its name in 1954 to *Printing World*, and the *British Printer* first appeared in 1888. Directories such as Kelly's *Directory of Stationers, Printers, Booksellers, Publishers and Paper Makers* (1872-) provide evidence of the increasing level of organisation of the industrry. The 1890s saw a series of additions to the list of trade periodicals and annuals, including the *British Lithographer* (1891-5), the *British Art Printer* (1895-) and, peraps the most famous of all, the *Process Work Year Book* (1895-), which was shortly re-named (and remains) *Penrose's Annual*. The desire to agree and maintain national standards of typographic and printing practice is reflected in the publication of rules and guidelines for compositors and printers. The best known of these is *Rules for Compositors and Readers*, written by Horace Hart, who was Printer to the University of Oxford 1883-1915. Hart's *Rules*, as it is known, was first compiled and used in 1893, but it was not published for general use until 1904. It remains a widely-used guide to typographic practice.

The most important innovation in the printing of texts during the last quarter of the nineteenth century was un-

The printers' register No. 5, 1 November 1863. 24.5 x 19 cm.

KNOWLEDGE IS POWER.

THE PRINTING TIMES.

Vol. I.]   JANUARY 1, 1873.   [No. 1.

TO OUR READERS.

WE have no desire to unduly obtrude our own personality; but, in introducing ourselves for the first time to what we hope will prove to be an ever-widening circle of readers, we think it right to state very briefly why we have come into existence, and what are the ends which we purpose to achieve.

The PRINTING TIMES is launched because it is thought that it will supply a well-defined and long-felt want. We have no disparaging word to say of our trade contemporaries. They fulfil, and fulfil ably, a distinct function of their own, with which we have no desire to interfere. But we believe —and we have abundant reason to know that we are not alone in the belief—that an independent journal is required which shall, so to speak, draw all the various branches of the Printing trade into one focus, and become not only their record of events, but their organ of inter-communication on all trade topics.

This is the gap in press journalism which we propose to fill. We shall spare no effort to make the PRINTING TIMES a complete and trustworthy monthly compendium of trade news from all parts of the world. We shall deal with all questions which may arise, either between any of the various branches of the trade, or within any given branch itself, with all fairness and frankness. Moreover we shall willingly throw open our columns to the full and free discussion of all such questions by the parties who are more or less immediately interested in them.

It is obvious that in an undertaking of this kind, we must rely to a considerable extent upon the co-operation of our readers. We have no wish that the PRINTING TIMES should be the organ of ourselves; we desire to make it the organ of the printing and all affiliated trades. Suggestions, items of news, correspondence, and all cognate matter, therefore, will be gladly received and put to the best practicable use for the benefit of the constituency whom we desire to serve.

In the absence of such a constituency—for of course we cannot secure co-operation until we have obtained readers—our present number must be taken as being rather an indication of the course we intend to pursue, than a specimen of what we hope to do in the future. But once surrounded by friends, upon whose assistance we can depend, we are confident that we shall be able to make the PRINTING TIMES a journal worthy of the trades of which it aspires to be the organ.

Having said this much, we retire at once into the obscurity of the editorial impersonality, trusting that we shall not again have to emerge from it till we can assure our readers that we have achieved at their hands the success which it will be our constant endeavour to merit.

THE FUTURE OF THE PENNY PRESS.

THE Penny Press, especially in the Provinces—to which, in this article, we intend to confine ourselves—is struggling with grave difficulties just now. In the public mind its price is irrevocably fixed. Other commodities, where the demand is equally uniform, are allowed to fluctuate in price according as the cost of production increases or diminishes; but with the daily provincial newspaper, a penny is as much considered its unalterable equivalent as five pounds are considered the unalterable equivalent of a five-pound note. The penny paper has become an institution. To change its price to a penny-farthing or three-halfpence, as you would any other article which you could no longer afford to sell for a penny, would be looked upon as little less than a revolution. Nevertheless, during the few years which have elapsed since the penny press came into existence, the cost of its production has gone up by from thirty to forty per cent., and at no time more rapidly than within the last two years. The growth of the institution, by extending the demand, has augmented the value of the literary labour employed upon it. The extension of sub-marine and continental telegraphy has sent up the cost of foreign news. The growing demand for "latest" and "special" intelligence, and the improved facilities offered by the postal telegraphic

1

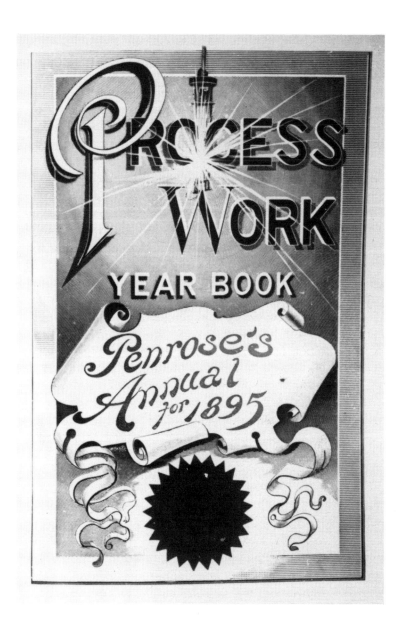

Process work year book, 1895. 24.8 x 34 cm.

doubtedly the invention of effective and dependable type composing machines, which made possible much greater speeds of setting type. There were two main models, both very successful in different ways. The Linotype composing machine, invented by Ottmar Mergenthaler (1854-99), a German living in America, worked on the principle of assembling matrices or moulds of types which were automatically justified and from which lines of type, known as slugs, could be cast. Mergenthaler completed his first machine in 1885 and in 1890 a much-improved version was available. Tolbert Lanston (1844-1913) was at the same time working on a different principle which led in 1889 to the invention of the Monotype composing machine. Unlike the Linotype machine, the Monotype had only one matrix for each character. The operator worked at a keyboard which in turn perforated a paper ribbon rather like a pianola roll, and this paper ribbon transmitted the operator's keyboard work to the casting function of the machine, which produced lines of single types, justified and ready for proofing. Both the Linotype and the Monotype companies published periodic reports which promoted their products amongst printers; these products included not only the composing machines, but also ranges of new or re-designed type faces which were available for use with the machines. *Linotype Notes* first appeared in 1897, and *The Monotype Recorder* in January 1902.

One of the most capable and prolific authors on printing during the last quarter of the nineteenth century was John Southward (1840-1902). Southward was born in Liverpool, the son of a printer. After working for his father and becoming involved with local journalism he came to London to improve his knowledge of typography, working in the meantime as a reader for two large publishers. Southward soon earned a reputation as a leading authority on printing, and his *Dictionary of Typography and Its Accessory Arts* (1871), which was first published as monthly supplements to *The Printer's Register*, became a highly respected reference work.

The Passing of the — Line Hand.

IT always was inevitable. So mechanical as set as the setting and spacing of a line of uniform type was bound to be accomplished by machinery, sooner or later, and the revolution is now being quietly effected in thousands of printing offices in all parts of the world.

The Opportunity of the Display Hand.

DOES this mechanical line-setting imply that the hand compositor's occupation is gone? By no means. It is instructive to find his higher and truer avocation in that of an artist in type. As a line-setter he cannot hope to compete with the machine operator. But as a display hand he has so fine a field open to him as any handicraftsman can command.

What has brought it all about?

THERE is only one answer to this:

The Linotype Composing Machine,

which is, compared with hand composition, what the web-printing machine is to the hand press, and what the sewing machine is to the seamstress's needle.

THE LINOTYPE COMPANY LIMITED,

189, FLEET STREET, LONDON, E.C.

Linotype Notes

No. 20   APRIL, 1899.   GRATIS.

All communications to be addressed to

THE EDITOR,
LINOTYPE NOTES,
188, Fleet Street,
London, E.C.

A copy of LINOTYPE NOTES as issued will be forwarded free to Users, Operators, and others who will send us their names and addresses.

We are this month issuing as a supplement to LINOTYPE NOTES a reprint from *The Stationer, Printer and Fancy Trades Register*, of a review on a powerful Linotype article, entitled "In the Steps," which we think will be interesting to our readers. In the opening chapter of this work the writer lays it down, staunch and dying (many-compositor enters a fashionable church, and calmly and without passion tells the congregation that his handwriting can live through the Linotype machines, adding, gatherically, "I'm not complaining, am I?" and then proceeds to add specially what those would do could he return to our artificial so-called Christian social system.

The following is an extract from an article in the *Bombay Advocate* describing the installation of Linotype machines now at work in that office:—"The clean appearance of this type, combined with the fact that the men who have worked at them for years have had no occasion to ever saw a Linotype before, and are to all effects and purposes raw apprentices, will convince the readers of the *Advocate* that the suggestions that no "hot side" this with the times, by the introduction of a Linotype installation.

The New York Typographical Union's fiftieth anniversary will occur in 1900, and it is suggested that the event be celebrated by a printing exposition, to would be shown printing devices, machinery, type, books, the manufacture of paper, the publishing of a daily Lino-

type, proverb, bookbinding, ink-making, and all matters appertaining to the trade. Old-time methods and antique specimens in comparison with modern would serve to show the immense advance in the art, and the influence on civilisation, forming an attractive feature to the general public. The project would be best if V.S. has a membership of 5,300 members, comprising much talent in various ways, so say nothing of the machine grouped under the allied trades.—*Ireland Printer.*

The members of the Middlesborough Branch of the Typographical Association have issued a request to the master printers of Middlesborough asking for an advance of the present minimum wages of journeymen, jobbing, and news printers in the town. The advances asked for 2s. per week and news hands 1¼d. per hour. The present position differs to be 32s. per week and news hands 30d. per hour. The overtime rate of the day, with an uniform minimum of the printing trade, in the opinion of the memorandum, is one of the reasons inviting the men that the time is approaching for making an appeal for increased remuneration.

The hon. secretary of the London District Institute of Journalists has received a letter from the general manager of the South Eastern and Chatham and Dover Railways announcing that a new train will leave Ludgate Hill at 2.30 a.m. on its journey at all stations except Penge East. The train leaving Ludgate Hill at 4.15 a.m. for Nunhead will be run on to Catford, calling at Crofton Park.

Another Linotype machine has been installed by Messrs. Parkinson and Blacow (Oldhaven). They inform us they are for jobbing work. They inform us they could produce machine-set work that would surprise many prejudiced printers.

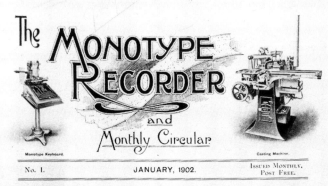

No. 1.   JANUARY, 1902.   ISSUED MONTHLY,
                                                  POST FREE.

THE MONOTYPE RECORDER.

In introducing the first number of this little pamphlet to our readers we will frankly admit that it is an advertisement, but it is by no means a mere puff of the "Monotype." It aims at giving the printers of the United Kingdom a ready means of estimating the progress made by the most highly perfected mechanical composer on the market, and of deciding whether it has come within the range of "practical politics" from their point of view or not.

With this object a note of all items of interest referring to the capability of the machine or to the success achieved by the Companies exploiting it will be found from month to month.

A page of composition of more or less difficulty showing the diverse uses to which the composer may be put will appear regularly, and in addition, as the Lanston Monotype Corporation are always at work cutting new faces, the latest product added to the stock and ready for delivery will be shown on the third page.

The RECORDER will help to keep users of the "Monotype" in touch with the Corporation and will contain hints as to the solution of those small difficulties which inevitably crop up from time to time in the case of all machines recently introduced to a new office, where the operators must necessarily be more or less strange to their work.

Opportunities will be made for assisting the ever growing number of those enterprising printers who have already adopted the Monotype by suggesting methods of raising the efficiency of their installations and increasing the production obtained from them.

In fine, the RECORDER will be made as useful to its readers as the space afforded by its columns will permit, but these columns will be rigorously kept within their present bounds so that the printer's valuable time will not be unduly encroached upon.

The Monotype has "come to stay" and the interests of the Corporation owning the rights in this invaluable invention (or, more properly speaking, inventions) will be pushed in a straightforward manner. The Corporation has something to sell which the printer only needs to see in practical work to appreciate. The Corporation asks nothing more than to have the capabilities of the machine tested, and, if found to be superlative, that the machine should be adopted. All they desire is that the Monotype shall have "a fair field and no favor," and that printers will refuse to be beguiled, by temporarily cheap offers of rivals, into doing their quota towards keeping a better machine permanently off the market.

As this is the first issue of this brochure it may be permissible to give a slight sketch of the history of the Lanston Monotype—to give the machine its full name.

The Monotype came from that ever prolific birthplace of inventive genius and its product, the United States, in 1897. The primæval stage goes back to the earlier "Eighties," and has now become buried in the "misty past;" but in 1897, on its arrival here, it might be called in its mediæval state. The keyboard was a mechanical one with but 132 keys, and the caster which was built by "hand" (i.e., without jigs, templates, or other standard tools) was only capable of manipulating the same number of matrices.

Since that period three great changes have taken place—firstly, the fount was raised from 132 to 225 matrices, involving changes on both caster and setter; secondly, the mechanical board was superseded by a vastly superior pneumatic board, giving wider measure, greater speed, and less liability to derangement; and thirdly, the caster was improved not only in the details of design of some of the important working parts, mainly directed towards increasing the life of the machine and securing greater perfection

Composed and Cast on the Monotype.

The *Monotype recorder* No. 1, Jan. 1902. 30.7 x 24 cm.

His *Practical Printing* (1882) appeared in many revised editions and became a standard textbook. *The Bibliography of Printing*, which appeared in three volumes 1880-6 under the names of Edward Clements Bigmore and C. W. H. Wyman drew heavily on Southward's knowledge and expertise, and he contributed numerous learned articles to reference works such as *Encyclopaedia Britannica* and *Chambers' Encyclopaedia*. One of the most useful sources for the modern reader is Southward's *Progress in Printing and the Graphic Arts in the Victorian Era* (1897)†, which contains a wealth of illustration as well as an informative and illuminating text. Two other useful reviews of the history of printing are K. Faulmann *Illustrirte Geschichte der Buchdruckerkunst* (1892) and the issue of *The Times* of 10 September 1912, which celebrated the paper's 40,000th number by publishing fifty monographs on printing, later re-published as a book.

As I have indicated above, periodicals about art played an important role in the dissemination of ideas, information and tastes about graphic art. Although many of them were dull in design and content, they often contained articles on graphic art and occasionally original prints of lithographs or etchings. In addition to those already mentioned, one may note magazines like *Annals of the Fine Arts* (1816-20), *L'Artiste* (1831-1904), *Art Union* (1839-1849) which changed its name to *Art Journal* (1849-1912), *Gazette des beaux arts* (1859-) and the *Magazine of Art* (1878-1904). This is not the place to discuss such publications in detail, but some further references will be given later.

Periodicals on art and design were mainly bought and read by a section of the middle classes that prided itself on its discrimination and taste. The same public responded to the work of the Arts and Crafts Movement, which became so influential in Britain and internationally from the 1870s to the end of the century. Perhaps the most important event in relation to graphic art and design was the founding of the Kelmscott Press by William Morris in 1891. William Morris

(1834-96) came to printing late in life, having spent most of his career as a designer working on the production of furniture, wallpapers, and similar domestic accessories. *A Note by William Morris on his Aims in Founding the Kelmscott Press* (1898)† is a succinct expression of his objectives in regard to printing. Two periodicals which also represent the Arts and Crafts spirit are *The Century Guild Hobby Horse* (1884-92) which became *The Hobby Horse* (1893-4), and *The Dial*, which appeared in three numbers between 1889 and 1893.

The Arts and Crafts impetus was taken over and given a rather more commercial and popular character by *The Studio* which appeared in 1893. *The Studio* contained numerous articles on illustration, letter form and other aspects of graphic communication; one of its most prominent contributors was Joseph Pennell. An invaluable guide to the contents of the early *Studio* is the *General Index* to the first twenty-one volumes 1893-1901, published in 1911. This was followed in 1908 by an index to the second twenty-one volumes 1901-8. In addition to the content of the monthly magazine, *The Studio* was also responsible for publishing a large number of anthologies of graphic art, many of them edited by the magazine's first owner, Charles Holme. Of special note is *Modern Pen Drawings: European and American* (1901), *Modern Etching and Engraving* (1902) and *Art in Photography* (1905), all edited by Holme.

The Studio tended to be rather conservative and perhaps a bit dull in design in comparison with its foreign equivalents which appeared during the 1890s. The most important of these are the Berlin Magazine *PAN* (1895-1900), the Munich *Jugend* (1896-1933) and the Viennese *Ver Sacrum* (1898-1903). *PAN*, and especially *Ver Sacrum*, contained graphic work of outstanding quality and power. The origins of art periodicals in German-speaking Europe has been dealt with in E. H. Lehmann *Die Anfänge der Kunstzeitschrift in Deutschland* (Leipzig, 1932). Works dealing with selected magazines

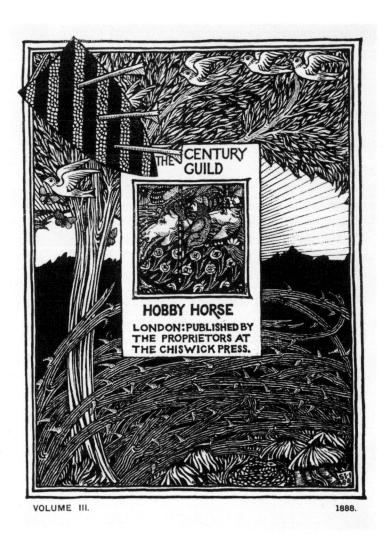

The Century Guild hobby horse Vol. III, 1888. Cover, 30.6 x 23 cm.

Ver Sacrum, Vol. I, No. 2, February 1898. Cover, 29.5 x 28.5 cm.

include G. Bott *Bildende Kunst 1850-1914: Dokumentation aus Zeitschriften des Jugendstil Pan. 1895-1900* (Berlin, 1970), K. H. Salzmann 'PAN — Geschichte einer Zeitschrift' in *Imprimatur* 1950-1951 pp.163-176, and C. M. Nebehay *Ver Sacrum 1898-1903* (Wien, 1975). A brief but useful guide to the history of art periodicals is provided in Trevor Fawcett and Clive Phillpot (ed.) *The Art Press. Two Centuries of Art Magazines* (1976).

Graphic communication was one of the last areas of design to attract the attention of the Arts and Crafts Movement, and by the close of the nineteenth century the reform of typography had little more than commenced. To modern eyes, even many of the best examples of late nineteenth-century printing look turgid and over-ornamented. By the first decade of the twentieth century there was widespread evidence of a major reform of letter-form and typography, and this reform was fed by two contrasted impulses—a revivalist impulse which was characteristic of the English-speaking world, and a more radical, even iconoclastic impulse which we find in Continental, especially German, typography.

A seminal figure in this period of reform was the scribe and calligrapher Edward Johnston (1872-1944). At the age of seventeen Johnston obtained a copy of W. J. Loftie *Lessons in the Art of Illuminating* (1885), a book which inspired him to make calligraphy his life work. W. R. Lethaby, one of the leading figures of the Arts and Crafts Movement, advised Johnston to study manuscripts at the British Museum. This he did, complementing it with the study of ancient inscriptional forms, notably the cast of lettering from Trajan's Column then housed at the Victoria and Albert Museum. From these inanimate sources Johnston resuscitated the living art of calligraphy, re-discovering for himself all the skills of preparing pens and other materials and the construction of letters. He was an influential teacher at both the Central School of Art and the Royal College of Art, his pupils including Eric Gill and T. J. Cobden-Sanderson. Johnston's most important publication was *Writing & Illuminating & Lettering* (1906), a manual which is so balanced and comprehensive that it has been described as 'almost beyond praise'. In spite of his strong historicist tendency, Johnston designed in 1916 a sanserif typeface for use on the London Underground Railway which had a major influence on subsequent British and Continental sanserif faces.

The revivalist tendency in typography was reinforced by several publications on the history of the subject, the most important of which was *Printing Types: their History, Forms and Use* (Harvard, 1922) by the American Typographer Daniel Berkeley Updike (1860-1941). Updike's book remains a standard text for the study of typography.

Johnston's former pupil Eric Gill (1882-1940) became a significant influence on the development of typography, especially in Britain. Gill's range of activities was much wider than Johnston's, embracing sculpture, illustration and monumental lettering as well as calligraphy and typography. He designed ten printing types, the best known being the roman Perpetua and the sanserif Gill Sans. Gill's book *An Essay on Typography* (1931)† is typical of his views on life and art, emphasising as it does the close bond which he felt existed between the qualities of art and design and the health of society.

One other individual who should be mentioned in connection with the typographic revival in Britain is Stanley Morison (1889-1967). Morison was responsible for supervising the redesigning of a type face for *The Times* newspaper, which appeared in 1930 as Times New Roman and has since become perhaps the most widely used roman alphabet in the English-speaking world. In 1922 Morison was a founder member of the Fleuron Society, an association dedicated to the improvement of typographic art. Its periodical *The Fleuron* (1923-30) provided a model of excellence for many other similar periodicals, notably *Signature* (1935-1954) edited by Oliver Simon, and *Typography* (1936-), which became *Alphabet*

THE FLEURON

A JOURNAL OF TYPOGRAPHY

EDITED BY OLIVER SIMON

NUMBER ONE

LONDON

At the Office of THE FLEURON

1923

The Fleuron, 1923. Title page, 27.6 x 21.5 cm.

and Image (1946-1948). In 1930 *The Fleuron* published
Morison's essay 'First Principles of Typography'†, a succinct
and personal account of the subject.

While the revival of typography in Britain took a rather
conservative character, on the Continent it was much more
radical. For a number of reasons too complex to deal with
here, many Continental designers desired a complete revolution in the language of graphic communication and the
creation of a new approach which had no historical or specific
national overtones. One of the leading figures of what became
known as The New Typography was the German designer
Jan Tschichold (1902-1974). Like Johnston, Tschichold was
inspired as a young man by the beauty of traditional calli-
graphic forms, and spent a great deal of his time studying and
re-creating them in his own work. However, he came to the
view that lettering and typography, and indeed the whole of
graphic communication, needed a new look which served the
needs of the modern world and was not encrusted by the
traditions and ornaments of the past. His book *Die neue
Typographie* (*The New Typography*) (Berlin, 1928)† was a
powerful and persuasive expression of this belief. Unfortunately, it was never published in English and remains rather
rare and difficult to obtain.

In due course Tschichold retreated from this extreme
modernist position, which he came to regard as unnecessarily
doctrinaire and authoritarian, and in his later work and writ-
ings he reverted to a more conservative approach, although
always guided by impeccable taste. The radical spirit of reform
was continued by several designers who studied or taught at
the Bauhaus design school, which was founded in Weimar in
1919 and closed in 1933. One of these, Herbert Bayer
(1900-) was a student at the Bauhaus 1921-1923. He
returned as a teacher 1925-1928, during which time he had a
major influence on typography and advertising. In its most
extreme form, The New Typography demanded the abolition
of capital letters, which were regarded as a historical ana-

JAN TSCHICHOLD

DIE NEUE TYPOGRAPHIE

EIN HANDBUCH FÜR ZEITGEMÄSS SCHAFFENDE

BERLIN 1928

VERLAG DES BILDUNGSVERBANDES DER DEUTSCHEN BUCHDRUCKER

Jan Tschichold *Die neue Typographie* 1928. Title page,
20.6 x 14.2 cm.

chronism, and the predominant or exclusive use of the new sanserif faces, which were thought to be free of historical and specific cultural connotations and therefore in keeping with the needs of the modern age. The German trade magazine *Gebrauchsgraphik* (1925-), later renamed *Novum Gebrauchsgraphik* published numerous articles about the new spirit in graphic communication and was widely read by typographers, printers and designers.

The influence of movements in the fine arts, painting and sculpture, can be seen in much of the work of the 1920s and 1930s. Cubism, Dada and Surrealism all evolved styles of representation which could be adapted by the graphic designer, such as the use of collage, photomontage and asymmetry. A fascinating example of this response to the fine arts is A. Tolmer *Mise en page* (1931), which contains a collection of graphic inventions using a wide range of styles deriving from contemporary painting and sculpture.

Attempts to examine characteristics of type faces such as their legibility date back at least as far as the late eighteenth century. During the 1920s the relatively new science of psychology came to have a closer bearing on the study of graphic communication. In addition to the question of legibility, psychologists became interested in the way in which type faces could suggest certain qualities, quite apart from their ability to convey a literal message. One of the earliest of these studies, an article by Anna Berliner entitled 'Atmosphärenwert von Drucktypen' ('Atmosphere-value of type faces'), appeared in the *Zeitschrift für angewändte Psychologie* in 1920, and the expression 'atmosphere-value' was subsequently adopted to denote the peculiar ability of type faces to convey certain emotional or psychological overtones.

The study of graphic communication from a scientific basis was much stimulated by the demand for systematic and effective advertising. Several psychologists and social scientists turned their attention to the examination not only of type

Cover of *Gebrauchsgraphik* Vol. I, No. 11, 1924. 30.6 x 22.5 cm.

A. Tolmer *Mise en page* 1931. Title page, 27 x 21 cm.

faces, but the effects of different kinds of layouts, colours, imagery, and design. An interesting early example is H. L. Hollingsworth *Advertising and Selling* (New York, 1923). Hollingsworth's book, however, was excelled and displaced by H. E. Burtt's extremely comprehensive *The Psychology of Advertising* (Boston, 1938)†, still one of the most thorough attempts to examine the process of advertising from a scientific point of view.

In the same year as Burtt's book, another publication appeared which more or less superseded all previous attempts to analyse type faces from a completely dispassionate and scientific standpoint, that is, one which was not related to aesthetics or to functional value in, for example, advertising. This was *Legibility, Atmosphere-Value and Forms of Printing Types* (Leiden, 1938)† by G. W. Ovink. In the USA the leading figure in the systematic study of every detail of typographic communication and reading was Miles A. Tinker, whose numerous publications include articles such as 'Legibility and eye movements in reading' (*Psychological Bulletin*, 24, Nov. 1927, pp.621-639) and, more recently, *The Bases for Effective Reading* (University of Minnesota, 1965). In Britain, the study of legibility was pursued in special relation to education and the problems of learning to read. A leading figure in this field of investigation was the psychologist Cyril Burt (not to be confused with the American Burtt), whose *A Psychological Study of Typography* appeared in 1959. One of the most concrete results of the movement for the investigation and reform of typographic communication was the creation of the Initial Teaching Alphabet (ITA) adopted in many British primary schools during the 1960s. J. Downing *The Initial Teaching Alphabet Explained and Illustrated* was published in 1964.

Improved ease of travel, which is a notable feature of life in the twentieth century, has meant that an increasing number of people find themselves spending periods of time in areas, the local language of which they do not understand. Under

LEGIBILITY, ATMOSPHERE-VALUE AND FORMS OF PRINTING TYPES

BY

Dr. G. W. OVINK

LEIDEN 1938
A. W. SIJTHOFF'S UITGEVERSMAATSCHAPPIJ N.V.

G. W. Ovink *Legibility, atmosphere-value and forms of printing types* 1938. Title page, 21.2 x 15 cm.

such circumstances, verbal notices and signs have limited value, and this is one factor which has stimulated the development of systems of pictorial communication which transcend language. Other factors which have encouraged the development of a reliable and rational pictorial language include the need felt by democratic governments to explain and persuade by means of statistical charts, graphs, etc., and the growing pressure to communicate with large populations of illiterate people in the developing countries. The most obvious manifestations of this tendency may be seen in the international standardisation of traffic signs, utility signs at airports, pictorial information about health precautions, and statistical presentations in official reports.

During the 1920s, parallel with the movement to reform and clarify typography, there appeared a movement to systematise pictorial language. A leading figure in this movement was the Austrian designer Otto Neurath (1882-1945), whose design team did much to stabilise and clarify the communication of information by means of schematic images which we may describe as pictographs. Neurath's system became known as ISOTYPE, a modified acronym for 'International System Of TYpographical Picture Education'. His book *International Picture Language. The First Rules of Isotype* appeared in 1936†.

Early writers on pictorial communication and print-making tended to confine their interest to issues such as the origin and provenance of works, the technical procedures surrounding their production, and the biographical background of the artist. An important exception to this rule is the nineteenth-century author P. G. Hamerton, who often attempted to discuss the nature of graphic imagery in more fundamental and analytical terms. This desire to bypass biographical and other contingent material and examine the physical character of prints and the way they are interpreted is revived in the work of the American William M. Ivins Jr., whose book *Prints and Visual Communication*

INTERNATIONAL PICTURE   LANGUAGE

THE   FIRST   RULES   OF   ISOTYPE

BY

OTTO   NEURATH

*Director of the International Foundation
for Visual Education, Writer of " Basic
by Isotype "*

WITH   ISOTYPE   PICTURES

LONDON:
BASIC ENGLISH PUBLISHING Co.,
45, GORDON SQUARE, W.C.1

Otto Neurath *International picture language* 1936.
Title page, 15.1 x 10.5 cm.

was published at Harvard in 1953. Ivins' book is not a 'scholarly' work in the sense of having masses of references marshalled in the support of a cool, scientific and rational argument; in some ways it is an intuitive and even emotional work. What the author attempted to do, relying on his extensive first-hand experience of fine prints, was to create a language for discussing the inherent physical qualities of prints and the likely impact of these qualities on the history of culture. Ivins coined the term 'syntax' to denote the graphic code which constituted the printed image, and this idea has since been widely adopted and used. Ivins' line of research is continued by Estelle Jussim *Visual Communication and the Graphic Arts* (New York, 1974).

During the early 1960s many new methods of analysis were applied to graphic communication, orginating in areas such as the social sciences and the study of cultural history. Perhaps the biggest single impact was made by the Canadian Marshall McLuhan, whose books *The Gutenberg Galaxy* (1962) and *Understanding Media* (1964) created something of a sensation. McLuhan argued that the technology of communication available to a given culture was not a mere transmitter of ideas and information, but played a crucial role in determining or even dictating what was transmitted. This notion was encapsulated in the aphorism of the 1960s, which became something of a cliché: 'the medium is the message'. Since the heyday of McLuhan's fame there has been a certain degree of scepticism about the correctness of his views, although much of what he said has in fact been assimilated to our culture and is reflected in the way we talk about communication, a case in point being his distinction between 'hot' and 'cool' media.

The analytical study of graphic communication in the context of cultural history has been continued most vigorously in the context of what is known as 'semiology', which is defined as the science of signs. Much of the output of the French author Roland Barthes, a leading semiologist, can be transferred to the study of graphic communication, as can the work of the Italian Umberto Eco, whose *A Theory of Semiotics* (Indiana, 1976) is one of the most important recent works on the subject. There have been few books which deal specifically with the semiological interpretation of graphic communication *per se*. A notable exception is Jacques Bertin *Sémiologie graphique* (Paris, 1967)†. Bertin's book is exclusively concerned with what he calls 'monosemic' imagery, that is imagery which is capable of only one correct interpretation (for example, maps, diagrams, graphs). He does not deal with what he calls 'polysemic' imagery (capable of more than one interpretation, such as figurative drawing and illustration) or 'pansemic' imagery (capable of an infinite number of interpretations, such as abstract painting). Nevertheless, Bertin's book is a milestone in the study of a major area of graphic communication. At the time of writing he is about to publish a further book, entitled *La graphique et le traitement graphique de l'information* (Berlin, New York, 1981), which will also appear in English.

A useful complement to these works from the mainstream of semiology is Nelson Goodman *Languages of Art* (Indianapolis, 1976). Goodman deals with a wide range of graphic categories, referring to such disparate phenomena as graphs, clock faces and old-master paintings, and he draws on a wealth of sources which include relevant research in psychology and art history. It is not an easy book to read, but repays careful and systematic study.

We usually take the classification of modes of graphic communication more or less for granted, but a closer examination suggests that the whole area of graphic communication can in fact be broken down into several groups or classes distinguished not so much in terms of their physical substance (e.g. paper, stone, visual display unit), but in terms of the general strategy adopted, regardless of its physical embodiment. A valuable attempt to classify and group these modes is Michael Twyman 'A schema for the study of graphic language', which appeared in *Processing of Visible Language* Vol. I, ed. Paul A. Kolers *et al*, (New York and London 1979).

This source book can of course cover only a tiny fraction, albeit, it is hoped, a representative one, of all the material on the subject. The student of graphic communication should learn to use the bibliographical and research tools which will provide further sources of information and ideas. These include the catalogue and subject index of the British Library and the National Art Library, the latter housed at the Victoria and Albert Museum. The *British Union Catalogue of Periodicals* (known as BUCOP) is invaluable for tracing the dates and locations of rare periodicals. In London two of the best libraries on the subject of printing are the St Bride Printing Library and the library of the London College of Printing. The art-historical index *Art Index* contains a proportion of entries relevant to graphic communication, principally in relation to print-making. Many of the most prominent British figures in the history of printing and publishing are to be found in the *Dictionary of National Biography*. Handy reference works which are widely available are G. A. Glaister *Glossary of the Book* (1960), W. Turner Berry and H. Edmund Poole *Annals of Printing* (1966) and Colin Clair *A Chronology of Printing* (1969). The rise of interest in the history of design has stimulated the publication of *A Bibliography of Design in Britain 1851-1970* (1979) by Anthony J. Coulson, which contains a lengthy and useful section on graphic design.

C. Stower

The Printer's Grammar

1808. pp. 141-143, 339-341

Observations on Composing.

Having arrived at that part of our work which more immediately concerns the young beginner, we shall now set out with making a few observations on the position or attitude he should endeavour to acquire at case, on his first introduction to that part of the business. This does not appear to have been of sufficient importance to arrest the attention of former writers on this subject, yet so great is the evil resulting from falling into improper habits at first, that nothing but a determined perseverance in those who have experienced their ill effects can remedy them. Many men, now working in the trade, frequently reflect, and with much justice, on persons under whose care they were brought up, for omitting to check them in those ill-becoming postures which produce knock knees, round shoulders, or other deformities. It is to be regretted that those who undertake so important a charge, as the instruction of youth in the first rudiments of the art, are not better qualified, or do not bestow on their trust a greater attention.

What to a learner may appear fatiguing, time and habit will render familiar and easy; and though to work with his cases on a level with his breast may at first tire his arms, yet use will so inure him to it, that it will become afterwards equally unpleasant to work at a low frame. His perseverance in this mode must be strengthened by the reflection that it will effectually prevent his becoming round shouldered, a distinguishing mark by which compositors are in general known, especially if they are above the common stature. This method will likewise keep the body in an erect position, and prevent those effects which result from pressure on the stomach.

The standing position should be easy, with the feet not too much apart; neither should the idle habit of resting one foot on the bed of the frame be encouraged, or standing with one foot bent inwards, the certain forerunner of deformity. The head and the body must be kept perfectly steady, the arms alone performing the operations of distributing and composing.

The question still remains undecided with many masters, as to the most proper part of the business that should first engage the attention of the learner without confusing his ideas; various methods are adopted, each following the mode he thinks best. Sorting pie is generally the first employment, and afterwards to set it up again, which unquestionably gives them a strong insight into the nature of the business, makes them acquainted with the different sizes of type and the method of composing, and prepares their understanding for the comprehension of whatever direction may be given them when they are put to the case. We shall, however, follow the method generally adopted, which is that of first teaching him the nature of the cases, a knowledge easily acquired by attention.

Since the very general introduction of round, in the room of long s's, many cases have been made upon a plan different from the original ones. It will not, perhaps, be improper here to give a sketch of those which have been adopted in many respectable printing-offices in London.

Some remarks were made above upon a scale lately produced by Lord Stanhope, wherein he proposes an alteration in the shape of the letter f, in order to do away the use of the present double letters, and to adopt others; our observations upon that alteration have likewise induced us to insert the plan of a pair of cases, in which the double letters are completely exploded. The utility of this plan we have already pointed out in the page referred to, fully convinced, that could the eye accustom itself to the proposed altered shape of the f, and were double letters relinquished altogether, the advantages that would result both to the employer and journeyman would exceed what we have before stated.

* * * * *

Practical Directions to Pressmen.

Careful, ingenious, and sober pressmen must stand high in the estimation of every master-printer. This character is easily acquired by well-disposed men; yet it is to be lamented, that few endeavour to merit an appellation so desirable. We shall now lay down a few directions, which, if properly attended to, will, we are persuaded, enable the pressman to do credit to himself, and justice to his employer, as well as to uphold and preserve that superiority which now so eminently distinguishes the British press.

Of putting up a Press.

An understanding pressman should know not only how to direct a printer's joiner to set up and fasten a press when it is made, but also how to give a strange joiner and smith instructions to make a press, perfect in all its parts, and in a symmetrical proportion, to any size.

This knowledge every pressman should be anxious to obtain, as he would then be able to detect and mend those accidents and defects which frequently happen in the common press; we therefore recommend particularly to his attention, the foregoing description of the parts of the common press, which will give him a thorough knowledge of its principles and operation.

The joiner having set together the frame, viz. the cheeks, feet, cap, head, till, winter, hind-posts, ribs, carriage, &c. the pressman directs, and sees him perform as follows:

Before the head is put into its place, the pressman rubs the whole tenoned ends and tenons well with soap or grease, and also the mortises the head slides in, and so much of the cheeks as the ends of the head work against, that it may the easier work up and down.

The feet must be placed upon an horizontal level floor, and the cheeks perpendicularly upright, the stays or braces placed so as the press may be kept in the most steady and stable position, as well as to give a check to the force of the hardest pull and most violent blow the bar may give by rebounding against the farther cheek, if by chance it slip out of the pressman's hand. This consideration may direct him to place one brace against the end of the cap that hangs over the near cheek, and in a range parallel with the fore and hind side of the cap: for the more a brace stands aslope to the two parallel sides, the less it resists a force offered to the end of them, viz. the near end of the cap, which is one main stay to the whole press. If he places another brace against the hinder corner of the farther end of the cap, it will resist the spring of the bar, when it may slip out of the pressman's hand; and placing two other braces, one against the near corner of the hind side of the cap, and the other against the farther corner of the fore side of the cap, the press will be sufficiently braced up, if the room will afford convenience to place the farther end of the braces against it.

By convenience, is meant a firm solidity to place the end of the braces against, be it either a stone-wall, brick wall, or some principal post, or a girder, &c. that will not start or tremble at the force of a pull. The braces ought to be straight, and of substance strong enough porportionable to their length; and, if possible, to be fixed in such a position that they may stand in the same straight line with the upper surface of the cap, viz. that the farther end of the brace neither falls lower or rises higher than the upper side of the cap. Neither ought the brace, though thus placed, to stand alope or askew, that is, make unequal angles with the side of the cap it is fastened to, but it ought to stand square, and make right angles with the respective sides of the cap; because in those positions the braces best resist the force of continued pulls.

But though this be, by the rules of architecture, the strongest, firmest, and most concise method for bracing up a press, yet the room the press is to stand in will not always admit of conveniences to place the braces thus; therefore the pressman ought to consider the shape of the room, both for the places to fit the braces to, and the positions to set the braces in; placing his braces as correspondent as he can to these rules.

The press being thus far fastened, the carriage is laid on; and if the joiner performs his part well in making the wood work, it will first lie exactly horizontal; if not, it must be altered where it is amiss, before the pressman can lay the stone, and before the stay of the carriage can be fitted under the end of the ribs.

John Johnson

Typographia

1824. vol. II pp. 500-502

On the Construction of Printing Presses.

The improved Presses were in general use throughout Holland, several years before their introduction into England, and the first change in their construction was wrought by an ingenious artist, named William Jansen Blaew, of Amsterdam, a man as famous for his excellent Printing, as for his Astronomical and Geographical productions. In the early part of his life he was employed as a joiner, but, having served out his time and being of an inquisitive disposition, he rambled to Denmark, about the period that the famous Tycho Brahe was establishing his Astronomical Observatory, by whom he was entertained, and under whose instructions he was employed in making Mathematical instruments, in which curious art he made very considerable improvements; this occasioned it to be generally reported, that all or most of the Sideral Observations published in Tycho's name, were the work of Blaew, as well as the Instruments with which they were made. Before these Observations were published to the world, Tycho, to gratify Blaew, gave him the copies of them, with which he went to Amsterdam, and there practised the making of Globes, according to those Observations. As his trade increased he was enabled to deal in Geographical Maps and Books, and became so particularly curious in his plates, that many of the best Globes and Maps were engraved by himself. He projected also a Universal Atlas, in the execution of which he engaged all the most celebrated geographers, and the best works of his time. It was published at Amsterdam, in 3 vols. folio, in 1638, in which year he died, aged 67; but his two sons, John and Cornelius, produced a new edition of his work in 1663, consisting of 14 folio volumes. When these books are found entirely coloured, they are both rare and valuable; as a fire destroyed a large portion of the stock of Blaew's sons. Jansen Blaew was likewise the author of a Treatise on the Gobes, and by his frequent Printing of books, he got such a knowledge of the practical part of the art, that he set up a Printing-House for the transaction of his business; wherein he soon found the inconveniencies attending the structure of the old Presses, which induced him to contrive remedies for every inconvenience, in which he succeeded so much to his expectation, that he caused nine new Presses to be made, each of which he called by the name of one of the Muses. As the excellence of these improvements soon became known to other Printing Houses, which induced their proprietors to follow Blaew's example, so that Presses of his structure became, in the course of a few years, almost general

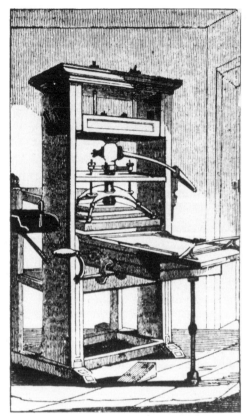

Press invented by Blaew.

throughout the Low-Countries, and from thence, of late years, notwithstanding the opposition of the ignorant, they have been introduced into England.

Improved Wooden Press.

It would have been impossible for our Readers to have formed any thing like a correct idea of the mechanism of Blaew's Press from the engravings heretofore given; we have endeavoured to obviate this difficulty in the foregoing subject, by representing it as clear as possible. In its construction, it differs very little from those of the present make, the most

material alteration appears to have taken place with respect
to the steadying of the spindle; that is, the crane, and likewise
the flange to which the plattin was attached, are removed,
and a square box, with a collar at the upper, and four hooks
at the lower end, are substituted; this box was made sufficiently hollow to admit the spindle to pass through it, the
toe of which entered into the cup placed on the plattin; it
passed through the till, and gave equal or more solidity to the
spindle, than the crane invented by Blaew. These Presses
(similar to the annexed engraving) have been in general use
in this country for more than the last century, and they would
most probably have remained so, had it not been for the iron
press invented by the late Earl Stanhope, an engraving of
which will be given in our next article; but no sooner had
these presses made their appearance, than several of the
Printers' Joiners and Smiths suggested to the Master Printers
the advantages to be derived from the addition of a compound
power attached to the wooden press; this suggestion was
embraced with avidity by several, and most of the others
speedily followed; but they were little aware of what they
were about; and in most instances they had done even worse
than nothing, for they were no sooner altered than they were
again out of repair, as some part or other generally gave way;
in truth, the Wooden Press was not calculated to bear the
extreme pressure thus applied, and not unfrequently this
power was attached by persons little capable of appreciating
the force of the leverage thus given. At this period about
half a dozen beautiful presses upon the French construction,
with long levers, which were pressed downwards, were in the
possession of three or four Master Printers of the Metropolis,
who, from the solicitation of these would-be connoisseurs in
presses, were induced to consent to have them altered according to the fancied improvements; but they were no sooner
put to work than the Masters found to their cost that they
had purchased a blank, rather than a prize; but it has ever
been, and still continues to be, the general practice of a

Improved wooden press.

majority of the Printers of the Metropolis, to adopt almost every new invention upon its first introduction; and many, we are firmly persuaded, have had too great reason to regret their over anxiety for new-fangled articles, before they were sufficiently in possession of their real qualities, whether good or bad.

T. C. Hansard

Typographia
1825. pp. 689-698

Printing Machines.

During the progress of this work hopes have been continually indulged that any delay in its publication would be compensated by finding the trade subsiding into something like a settled state, and enabling this chapter to be so far completed as to present a full account of the various machinery used in printing; but since the first application of the steam-engine to this business the inventive genius of the age has been particularly alive to the improvement of the art which is ultimately the improver of all others, and no sooner has a clear description, and satisfactory opinion been formed of one invention, than another has started into notice, with, of course, some pretensions to superiority over all those that have preceded it.

One general feature in the various inventions above referred to for improvements in (the speed of) printing, with the exception of one not yet generally known, is first the substitution of two cylinders, or of one cylinder and a plane, for producing the impression, instead of the two plane surfaces of the ordinary, or Stanhope press; and secondly, the use of cylinders covered with the adhesive and elastic composition, for applying the ink to the surface of the forme of types, as described in a preceding chapter, which, in the old process, was laid on with large balls, or dabbers.

For these important ideas both the public and the patentees of printing machines seem to be indebted to Mr. William Nicholson, the editor of the journal bearing his name, who obtained a patent for them in the year 1790. Upon referring to this patent, descriptions of which have been given in the

Repertory of Arts, the Pantologia, and other scientific works, it appears that Mr Nicholson has completely taken the lead upon this subject; and it is probable, that had he joined the actual practice of the art of printing by machinery to his knowledge of the theory, little would have been left for subsequent mechanicians to perform, and still less to be claimed as their original inventions.

Those parts of the specification relative to our subject, refer, first, to casting the type; secondly, to applying the ink. and thirdly, to taking the impression. The first of these relates to the formation of the mould, so as to cast two, three, or more letters at one pouring in of the metal; and to the finishing the stem of the letter, so that the tail is rendered "gradually smaller the more remote it is, or farther from the face. Such letter may be firmly imposed upon a cylindrical surface in the same manner as common letter is imposed upon a flat stone." . . . "To be imposed in frames or chases adapted to the surface of a cyliner of wood or metal." . . . . The ink, &c. is proposed to be applied by a cylinder covered with leather, pelts, &c. with "two, three, or more smaller cylinders, called distributing rollers, moving longitudinally against the colouring cylinder, so that they may be turned by the motion of the latter." . . . . The impression is designed to be effected by another cylinder causing the paper to pass between "two other cylinders, or segments, in equal motion, one of which has the blocks, forme, plate, assemblage of types, or originals attached to, and forming part of its surface, and the other is faced with cloth, or leather, and serves to press the paper, cloth, or other material, as aforesaid, so as to take off an impression of the colour previously applied." This he varies many ways, in the usual see-saw language of patents, applying his invention "to the printing of books in general, paper-hangings, floor-cloths, cottons, linens, silks, ribbons, laces, leather, skin and every other flexible material whatsoever." He then gives descriptions and drawings of the presses and apparatus to effect the intended purpose, either by means of the types, &c. fixed to the cylinder, or to formes, or plane surfaces submitted to the action of the cylinder by being laid on planks passed horizontally between them, the whole of which may be found, with the specification of the patent, in the work just referred to.

My reason for giving so detailed an account of a patent for printing machinery which, having been taken out upwards of thirty years ago, has so long since expired, is this: from the arrangement of his proposed colouring cylinder—of its subordinate, or distributing cylinders—of the impression cylinder—the plane table—the mode of catching up the paper and carrying it round the cylinder—the impression cylinder, whereby the paper is pressed against the type as that cylinder revolves, and by which means the sheet was to be printed— these, and many other parts of Mr. Nicholson's machine, as described in the specification, show that all subsequent attempts at machine-printing are but so many modifications of the same principle, rendered at last practicable by the invention of the composition for covering of balls and cylinders; without which, I risk nothing in saying, that no printing machine, at present invented, would ever have been rendered in the least degree effectual.

Again; Mr. Nicholson's idea (impracticable as I conceive it to have been in carrying on the various indispensable processes of proofs, revises, authors' corrections, &c.) of composing and imposing wedge-formed type, was in some measure modified and brought into practice by the pans, or galleys, of Mr. Bacon, fixed so as to form a rectangular frame, or prism, upon his cylinder, to revolve against one cylinder, or segments of cylinders, for inking, and another for pressure. And since Mr. Bacon, Applegath and Cowper's stereotype plates, cast or bent to form segments of a circle, so as to be fixed on a cylinder, are but substitutes for a like purpose.

The means, however, which Nicholson specified for distributing the ink were essentially defective; and the other parts of his invention were but very imperfectly carried into effect.

It is scarcely necessary to observe, that the great object in the employment of machinery is to lessen the expense of printing; and that the comparative merits of the various printing machines must be determined by this common and final standard.

In order to obtain this most important result, it is obvious that, in the construction of a machine, simplicity, durability, and a constant aptitude or readiness for working, are the first and most essential requisites; without which the most ingenious combination of mechanical knowledge, however highly to be esteemed as a piece of work, will produce little or no advantage to the proprietor or the public.

In the attainment of the above-mentioned requisites, one of the principal difficulties to be overcome is the equal spreading, or, as it is technically called, distribution, of the viscid and adhesive ink upon the face of the types, for which purpose very elaborate and costly apparatus has been made use of in other machines, and subsequently removed by the invention of the composition-covered cylinders. By this improvement, adapted to a printing machine, the perfect distribution of the ink appears to be attained by very simple means, and the same hue or shade of colour is preserved by the most trifling degree of attention, with a regularity which cannot be affected by the hand-rollers of the common class of workmen.

The engraving represents the elevation of a machine, worked by steam, or other competent power, for printing both sides of a sheet of paper, in which the sheet is conveyed from one cylinder to the other, by means of endless cords combined with a series of conveying cylinders, or drums.

The following little section will serve to give a general idea of the principle upon which these machines are constructed.

A is a cylinder, which gives the first, or white-paper impression. B, a similar cylinder, which gives the second impression, or iteration. C C C C, cylinders, or drums, over which the sheet of paper passes in firm contact, being held by

the pressure of endless strings; the sheet of paper ends at D, and comes out of the machine, printed on both sides, at E. The course of the strings and drums is indicated by the arrows.

The rollers for inking, in a machine of this construction, according to the last improvements of Mr. Cowper, lie horizontally upon a plane smooth surface, called a distributing table, in open notched bearings, acting by their own weight, and revolving by the friction of their surfaces against the surface of the table, without wheels, springs, or any other machinery whatever; so that, on the ground of simplicity and readiness for working, nothing can excel the contrivance.

The inking apparatus consists of an ink-trough, a plane surface, and rollers; the type passes under the rollers, G G G; the rollers, H H, assist in distributing the ink upon the surface of the distributing table, I, which is fed with ink from a trough on the spindle of the wheel, K, by means of a vibrating roller, which cannot be seen in the drawing.

The rotatory motion of the printing cylinders and drums is produced by a train of wheels at the back of the machine, and the distributing tables upon which the formes are placed move backwards and forwards under the cylinders A and B, and the rollers G G G, by means of a double rack, R, beneath the table.

The printing machines of König, Walters, Bensley, Applegath and Cowper, Donkin, Brightley, Rutt, Winch, Cooper and Millar, Congreve, Wood, Napier and lastly, My Own, all possess one and the same general principle, applied in a variety of forms. The formes, fixed on the carriages (the ink being communicated to the face of the type by an arrangement of rollers), are drawn under a cylinder, on which the sheet being laid, the impression is taken off on one side. The sheet is then conveyed to a second cylinder, by the rotation of which it is carried on to *the second forme*, or reiteration, and the sheet is perfected; or, to speak intelligibly to those who are not of the profession, the other side is printed. All the manual labour in this process, by those impelled by steam or other machinery, is performed by two boys, one of whom lays the paper on the first cylinder, while the other receives it from the second cylinder, and lays the heap perfectly even.

Mr. König was the inventor of the first steam-engine printing-machine brought to maturity in this country, and which he erected for Mr. Walters, proprietor of The Times newspaper. "Whether he was indebted to Mr. Nicholson for his elementary principles, or whether almost the same ideas spontaneously occurred to each individual, is a question that can only be satisfactorily solved by the former."

The Literary Gazette of October 26, 1822, contains a brief notice of the origin and progress of this invention, and its first application to the purposes of book-work, with an excellent perspective view of the machine. As I have been kindly offered the use of the engraving, I shall adopt the description also.

Mr. Bensley's Printing Machine.

"M. König, by birth a Saxon, and by occupation a printer, many years ago conceived it possible to print by steam, though he then expected no more than to be able to give accelerated speed to the common press, to which end his first efforts were bent. As from the nature of such an undertaking, considering the state of scientific pursuits in his native land, he could calculate on little success unaided by others, and failing in his application for encouragement and support at the hands of the most eminent printers in several of the continental capitals, he turned his eyes towards England. Arriving in London about 1804, he submitted his scheme to several printers of repute, who, not being disposed to incur the risk of property which a series of experiments were sure to incur, and perhaps placing little confidence in a successful issue, received his overtures very coolly; and it is probable his applications in this country would have shared the fate of similar attempts abroad, had he not finally been introduced to Mr. Bensley senior, who, attracted by M.K.'s plans, speedily entered into an arrangement with him. After a short course of experiments on the fabrication of a press which should have accelerated motion, and at the same time render the work of the man who inks the type unnecessary, the above gentlemen were joined by Mr. G. Woodfall and Mr. R. Taylor, the former of whom however soon retired. The remaining three, in no wise discouraged by the tediousness and expense which all who are conversant with the progress of any invention in machinery well know to be unavoidable, persevered amidst unforeseen perplexities, which were doubtless not diminished by the parties' deficiency in practical mechanical knowledge.

"It was at length discovered that the intended improvement of the common press could not be brought to bear; and that much labour and prodigious expense would be thrown away, unless more radical alterations were invented.

"Cylindrical printing was now thought of—and after some two or three years of renewed exertion, a small machine was brought forth, the characteristic of which was, that instead of the printing being produced by a flat impression (similar to the press) the sheet passed between a large roller and the types still flat; and in lieu of the old fashioned balls, used by

hand to beat over the types and so to communicate the ink
to their surface, skins were strained round smaller rollers, on
which it was contrived to spread the ink, and under which
the forme, *i.e.* the frame in which the types are fixed, passed
in its way to the printing cylinder. Considerable promise of
success attended this production; and after continued experiments it was deemed practicable to extend the general
principles to a more powerful machine. To print a newspaper
was considered highly desirable—and on exhibiting to Mr.
Walters, proprietor of the Times newspaper, the machine
already erected, and showing what further improvements
were contemplated, an agreement was entered into with that
gentleman for the erection of two large machines for printing
his Journal. So secret had been the operations of the patentees,
that the first public intimation of their invention was given to
the reader of The Times on Monday the 28th of November
1814, who was told that he then held in his hand one of
many thousand impressions thrown off by steam. At this
time but few persons knew of any attempt going on for the
attainment of the above object; whilst among those connected
with printing, it had often been talked of, but treated as
chimerical.

"The machines at the Times office, cumbrous and complicated as subsequent improvements have made them appear,
are yet, in many respects, admirably adapted to the purpose
for which they were erected, and it is believed will outlast
many contrivances for printing which have been since brought
out.

"The next advance in improvement was the manufacture
of a machine for Messrs. Bensley, distinguished from those
before mentioned, by the mode of perfecting (or printing on
both sides) so that the sheet of white paper is placed in the
feeder and delivered from the machine printed on both sides.
In addition to the essential difference between this machine
and those previously made, it came forth with many obvious
improvements, though still unquestionably complex: and for

the first attempt at effecting register (causing the pages to fall precisely on the back of one another) a greater degree of success than might have been expected was attained, subsequent experience showing the many difficulties to be surmounted in the accomplishment of this object. Deficiencies were now detected in the inking: the strained skins were found uneven in their surface; and attempts were made to clothe the rollers with an elastic preparation of glue, treacle, &c. which has at length attained perfection.

"By this time the invention had attracted the attention of various individuals, who thought the manufacture of printing-machines an easier task than they afterwards found it to be; and far the greater number of attempts, we believe, failed almost as soon as undertaken. A machine, however, similar in its capacities to that last mentioned, but much more simple in its construction, has been brought out—under the direction of some eminent English engineers. It was not long before these gentlemen were requested to apply their inking apparatus to Messrs. Bensley's machine; and at one stroke, as it were, forty wheels were removed—so great was the simplification: and at the same time the defects of the former system of communicating the ink to the types were most effectually remedied. Massive and complicated as it was, yet as an immense expense had been incurred in its erection, Messrs. Bensley went on using their machine until the destruction of their establishment, by fire, in 1819. And even after the re-building of the premises, the machinery, which had been only partially damaged, was reinstated, and worked for some time. It has now, however, given place to two large and admirable machines built on the improved plan, which, when inspected by a judicious eye, can only create wonder at the heretofore circuitous manner adopted to attain ends so apparently within easy reach. The writer has no hesitation in stating, that the original machine contains upwards of one hundred wheels; whereas the new machine, with about ten wheels, accomplishes, in point of quantity, exactly the same object, with a marked advantage in regard to the quality of the printing. Another important point respecting the new machine is, that it occupies scarcely half the space of the original one.

"The printing machine, in its present state, appears susceptible of little improvement. It produces excellent work, and its movements are attended with certainty and despatch —the double, or perfecting, machine throwing off 800 to 1000 sheets, printed on both sides, within the hour, and the single machine delivering 1500 or 1600 done on one side; which, in cases where one forme of the types (as in newspapers) is ready to be worked off while the last side is preparing, is attended with the greatest advantage, since the rate of delivery thereby becomes doubled. The first is that by which our Gazette is printed, and the last described is that with which Mr. B. Bensley is now (and has for a considerable time been) printing the Morning Chronicle newspaper.

"Other leading daily newspapers are also wrought off by steam; as well as several publications of extensive circulation. Like almost every ingenious invention, this has no small portion of prejudice to encounter, and perhaps has been longer in forcing its way than many other schemes of real utility. The various advantages, however, which it holds forth have attracted the attention of several proprietors of the more extensive printing concerns, who have introduced it with benefit to the public—to whom, by means of this great reduction of labour, the productions of the press may be furnished at a reduced rate of charge.

"In the engraving, a boy is represented as laying on A, the sheet of white paper. B, is the cylinder which prints the first side of the paper. C C, intermediate cylinders over which the paper travels to D, the cylinder which gives the final impression. E, the inking rollers under which the forme (*i.e.* the types) is in the act of passing. F, the reservoir of ink, from which the inking rollers are supplied. G, the forme, receiving its last inking before it goes under the printing

Perspective representation of Mr. B. Bensley's printing machine.

cylinder. H, a sheet is seen just being delivered into the hands of another boy, whose business it is to keep the sheets, as they come out, in a heap. The lines at top of the machine represent the tapes, which run round the cylinders and secure the sheet."—*Lit. Gaz. Oct. 26, 1822.*

C. H. Timperley

The Printers' Manual

1838. pp. 89-95, 102

Directions to Pressmen.

OF PRESSES.

Having endeavoured to lay before the young typographer the necessary information connected with the COMPOSITOR'S business, I shall now call his attention to that most important branch of the art—the PRESSMAN'S, (who may be called the actual printer,)—a branch which is the very end and consummation of all the compositor's previous care and labour—a branch which, if in the least degree neglected, will cause all the printer's pains and skill in display, all his expenses in beautiful type and accurate correctors, to be passed over disregarded; therefore careful, ingenious, and sober pressmen stand high in the estimation of every master printer.

The operations of the printing-press, when conducted by an expert pressman, are performed with a surprising rapidity; but the labour is very great. Two men are required to make a "full press," (when only one is at work, it is called "half press") who take it by turns to pull, that is, work the press; and beat or roll, that is, to ink the types. Whilst one man is employed in pulling the sheet, his comrade is distributing the ink on his balls or rollers, by applying them to the ink block, and the ink should be well spread out by the muller; if working with the roller, he should keep it in motion in varying directions, upon the plane surface of the table, whereby he obtains a perfectly equal coat of ink upon the face of the composition. By this time the other man having made the pull, run out the press, and opened the tympan, the other instantly begins the inking, whilst the puller gets the sheet changed; great care and attention is necessary on the part of the man who inks the types, for on him depends that regularity of colour which is so essential to the beautiful in typography. The advantages of the iron presses in working are very considerable, both in saving labour and time. The first arises from the beautiful contrivance of the levers, the power of the press being almost incalculable at the moment of producing the impression; and this is not attended with a correspondent loss of time, as is the case in all other mechanical powers, because the power is only exerted at the moment of pressure, being before that adapted to bring down the plattin as quickly as possible.

A new press should always be well employed for the first few months with heavy forms, and the pressmen ought to be particular in doing their duty, by taking care that they always keep on a sufficient power, and see that the bar be well pulled down. This is the only sure means of making it work free and well ever after: many a press has been spoiled by this neglect, and also that of working jobs at them before they are properly brought to their bearings. With the presses are sent practical directions to set them up, which a pressman should well attend to, so that at any time he may take them to pieces and clean them, which is of the utmost importance. Our space compels us to be as brief as possible; but the following list of presses will enable the reader to know the names at least of the principal ones which have been offered to the profession.

A printing press is a machine requiring very accurate mechanical construction. At the earliest period of the art it was conceived to be so perfect that no very material improvements took place in its make, until Lord Stanhope invented a press, constructed entirely of iron, from the general outlines of which, in all that have followed, the principle is essentially the same, and which press will ever bear the name of its inventor.

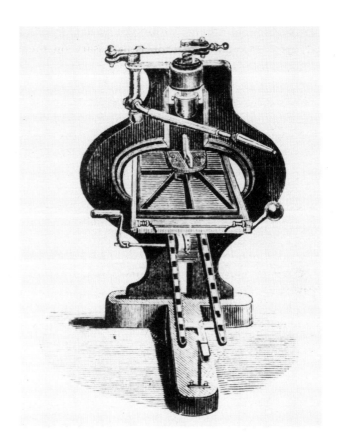

At the present day the old wooden press is nearly exploded, and therefore it would only be a waste of time to notice it; nor can I find space, but for those, which are very few, that possess all the requisites, for the purposes of printing, and repaying a master-printer for the great outlay. Lord Stanhope, with the assistance of Mr. Walker, an ingenious mechanic, introduced his press to public notice in the year 1800, and it has hitherto maintained its character for being well adapted for the purposes of printing; combining quickness with ease to the workman—evenness of impression—and durability and constant good condition. Lord Stanhope having objected to

the taking out of a patent for his invention, it was consequently thrown open, upon which several engineers and
smiths began to manufacture presses on the same principle;
it is true some of them made trifling alterations, but they
were scarce worth notice; therefore, in order to find a market
for them, they sold them somewhat cheaper; but those from
the original manufactory were infinitely superior. A representation of this press is given, which consists of the following
parts; the tee, staple, rounce, ribs, standard, main screw,
short head, arbor, top plate, long head, coupling bar, piston,
back plate, ears, balance weight, bar, plattin, table and
tympans. The first to deviate from the principles of the above
press, was a German of the name of D'Eighn, whose press was
known by the name of the SECTOR, which was much like
the Stanhopean in formation; a great objection to which
arises from the insecure manner of the *plattin*, which is by
no means so effectually secured as it ought to be. They have
a great quantity of ornamental brass work, which give them a
pleasing appearance to the eye; but it is not the glitter of
gaudy tinsel that a practical printer wants. D'Eighn afterwards
disposed of his patent-right to a person of the name of
Golding, who continued to manufacture them for some
time. He then invented another press, and soon afterwards
died, when his widow disposed of the patent to Mr. Cogger,
who entered into partnership with a Mr. Scott, and their
press was denominated the COGGER.

The next that came forward was Mr. Ruthven, a printer
of Edinburgh, whose press differed materially from all that
had preceded it, which he styled the RUTHVEN.

The next competitor for public favour was a person of the
name of Russell, whose press is manufactured by Messrs.
Taylor and Martineau, of London, and was denominated the
RUSSELL PRESS. These presses are simple and easy to work,
though apt to slur.

To the ingenuity and talent of Mr. George Clymer of
Philadelphia, we are indebted for the following press, which is

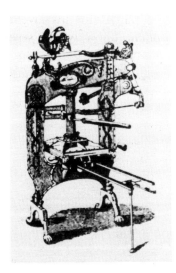

denominated the COLUMBIAN, who, after having manufactured a supply of them at home, arrived in this country,
in 1817, to introduce his press to the printers of Europe,
which had given such universal satisfaction to those connected with the art in America. The highly favourable, and
very flattering testimonials which Mr. Clymer produced on
his arrival in London, from the gentlemen connected with the
press in different parts of the United States, where they had
been in active operation, clearly evinced to the printers of
Great Britain and Europe, that his invention was well deserving
their countenance and encouragement; and, notwithstanding
they had presses not only of the Stanhopean manufacture,
but also of several others, yet the properties of Mr. Clymer's
Columbian press, supported by the above testimonials, were
the immediate cause of their introduction into several of the
first houses in the metropolis, and many of the others soon
followed; they were also introduced into several of the first
printing-offices on the continent.—This press is composed of
the following parts: the feet, staple, ribs, fore-stay, rounce,
main lever, elbow-piece, counterpoise lever, links, table,
plattin, piston, check or guide pieces, back bar, back-return

lever, shoulder piece, bar, connecting rod, eagle, &c. To increase the power, take out the small bolt in the middle of the shoulder piece, and turn the rod to the right—that is, take up the screw: to diminish it, turn the rod to the left, viz. lengthen the rod by unscrewing: the filed part of the eye must always be kept downwards.

Dr. Church's, a native of America, followed the Columbian press: his plan differed from every other; and it may be stated that he failed altogether in producing a press worthy of notice.

After the Stanhopean and Columbian presses, the meed of praise is due to the late R. W. Cope, of London, for his invention of the ALBION, which deserves to be placed in the first rank in the list of presses for power and ease to the workman in every point of view: first, they are much lighter in respect to weight of metal: secondly, the pull is very easy; notwithstanding which, it is equal in power to any of them, not even excepting the Columbian: thirdly, it is better adapted for expedition: fourthly, there are so few parts belonging to it, and consequently the machinery is in itself so simple, that there is not the least chance of their being put out of order, or liable to the least accident from wear: fifthly, the works being so simple, are all contained in the hollow of the piston, on which the power is given. This is the first instance of a hollow piston ever having been used for a press. Now manufactured by J. Hopkinson, Finsbury, London.

The next that came forward was Mr. Ruthven, a printer, at Edinburgh. He materially differed from all his predecessors: his press was styled the RUTHVEN. They unquestionably possess great power; but we object to these presses on account of the action of the bar, which is forced down by the pressure of the left, or by both hands. A man may sprain his wrist; or should his hand slip off, the rising of the bar would of course injure his arm between the latter and the press: also, from the very confined position of the works, it is almost next to an impossibility to oil or clean them without taking the press to pieces, which is a very troublesome and disagreeable operation.

Mr. Hope, of Jedburgh, in Scotland, was also the inventor of a press.

In 1820, Mr. Daniel Threadwell of the United States of America, came to England and took out a patent for a press, which was manufactured by Mr. Napier. In this press, the power necessary for giving the impression is obtained by means of a lever, or treadle.

The last, though not the least, in our notice of printing-presses manufactured in London, is that called the IMPERIAL PRINTING PRESS, invented and manufactured by Mr. J. Sherwin and J. Cope, and may justly vie with any of its competitors for ease, expedition, and durability.

THE BRITANNIA PRESS, invented and manufactured by R. Porter, of Leeds, in Yorkshire, is highly spoken of by many practical printers, and extensively patronized in the counties of York and Lancaster.

Many persons in different parts of the kingdom have

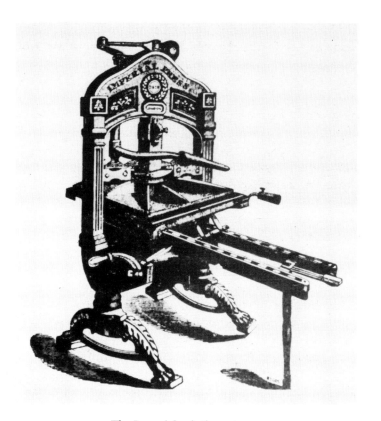

The Imperial printing press.

entered the lists as makers of iron presses; but, with very few exceptions, are they known beyond the vicinity where they are manufactured. The late Mr. Stafford, of Bingham, and his son and successor, have made some presses which are well thought of, though light, and consequently not adapted for heavy work. Their portable press is certainly deserving of support.

The invention of machinery, for the purposes of printing, first came into operation in England in the year 1814; and after many efforts, has now arrived at that state of perfection which seems to admit of no further improvement either for newspapers or for bookwork. To the ingenuity of Mr. König, a Saxon by birth, with the assistance of Mr. Bensley, Mr. Walters, and other eminent master printers, is the printing-trade indebted for this vast change in their professsion. These machines are now principally manufactured by Messrs. Cowper, of London and Manchester; by Mr. Napier, of London; and by a firm at Belper, in Derbyshire.

After all, in the great variety of forms and qualities of work passing through any printing-office, with the exception of newspapers, recourse must still be had to the aid of good manual presses and experienced pressmen. The serious expense of a printing-machine can only be repaid by execut-ing an extraordinary quantity of work in a much less portion of time than that usually occupied for the same work done by ordinary means. As, therefore, the time consumed in laying-on, or making ready a form, must be valuable in proportion to the number of sheets which might be struck off in that time; so, frequent repetition of the previous process for short numbers would counterbalance all gains arising from the speed in working. Machine printing will, therefore, be only applicable to works of extensive sale. But those of which limited numbers are printed; those also requir-ing a superior description of press-work with fine ink; fine and large paper copies, with alterations of margin; and many other peculiar circumstances which are continually occurring, will always require a judicious choice of men and materials, for the old mode of working, varied as circum-stances may at the moment require. Half-sheet work, or jobs printed on one side only, are either impracticable or disad-vantageous at a perfecting machine.

OF INKING TABLES.

With the removal of the old wooden press, and the invention of rollers, was also exploded the ink-block, for which was substituted frames or tables. These tables are manufactured by Cope, of London, and are composed wholly of iron, with the cylinder turned off to the greatest exactness, under which is a steel edge, that scrapes the ink off the cylinder to the exact quantity required: this is regulated by means of counterpoise levers that pass under the table, on which is hung two weights, to be removed according to the quantity of ink required for the work; one end of these levers are to press against the ductor, or regulator. The ductor and cylinder are fitted so close, that the latter will hold water; consequently there is not the least possibility of more ink escaping than is wanted for the purpose required. The cylinder has an ornamental cover, which is always kept on except when a fresh supply of ink is required; by which means all dirt and dust is kept both from the ink and cylinder: the latter is moved by a small handle at one end: the table is turned off in a lathe perfectly true, the same as in the presses.—In addition to the above invention, many other descriptions of tables are in use: frames with mounted tops of marble, lead, or hard wood: those of the latter kind are in most general use throughout the kingdom.

*   *   *   *   *

WETTING PAPER.

Paper is commonly wet in a trough lined with lead, full of clean water. The paper intended to be wet is placed on the left hand of the trough, and a paper board with its breadth before him on the right, laying first a wrapper or a waste sheet of paper on it, that it may not soil the first sheet of the heap. Then take up the first token, and lay it with the backs of the quires towards the right hand, that it may be caught more readily at the back of each quire with that hand, laying that token across the rest of the heap, that he may the easier know when he comes to the end of it. Take a quire by the centre of the back in the right hand, and the edge of it in the left, and lay it down upon the waste sheet, open it, and leave a few sheets. Having laid down this dry laying, take the remainder of the quire with the back of it in the right hand, and the edge of it in the left, as before, and closing the hand a little, that the quire may bend rather downwards between the hands, dip the back of the quire into the left hand side of the trough; and discharging the left hand of the quire, draw it through the water with the right; but as the quire comes out, quickly catch the edge of it again in the left hand, and bring it to the heap; and by lifting up the left hand, bear the under side of the quire of the dry paper, laid down before, lest the dry sheet should stick to the wet before the quire is placed in an even position, and so perhaps wrinkle a sheet or two, or else put a dry sheet or two out of their even position. But this drawing the quire through the water, is performed either quick or slow; if the paper be weak and spongy, perform it quickly; if strong and stubborn, slowly. To place this quire in an even position, lay the back of it exactly upon the open sheet of the former, and then let the side of the quire in the left hand fall flat down upon the heap; and discharging the right hand, bring it to the edge of the quire; and with the assistance of the left thumb, still in its first position, open or divide either a third or a half of the whole quire, according to the quality of the paper; and spreading the fingers of the right hand as much as possible through the length of the quire, turn over the open division of it upon the right hand side of the heap. Having wet the first token, double down a corner of the upper sheet of it on the right hand, so that the further corner may lie a little towards the left hand of the crease in the middle of the heap, and that the other corner may hang out on the near side of the heap, about an inch and a half; this sheet is called a token sheet, placed as a mark for the pressman, that he may know how many tokens the heap consists of. Having wet the whole heap, lay a wrapper or waste sheet of paper upon it, that the paper-board may not soil the last sheet; then take up as much water as you can in the hollow of the hand, and throw it over the waste sheet, that it may moisten and soak downwards into the unwet part of the last division of the quire. This is repeated three or four times. The paper being thus wet, the heap is removed upon the paper-board, and set by in a part of the room, appropriated for that purpose, and another board laid upon it; and upon the middle of the board is set about half a hundred weight, which remains for the purpose of pressing the heap, generally till next morning; as pressmen usually wet their paper after they have left work at night. All paper would be better if it were separated and turned in the course of the next morning, if it has been wet over night, and pressed again for seven or eight hours. Paper, or wetting boards, are made of deal to the sizes required; they should be kept solely for that purpose, and by no means allowed to be used to unlock forms upon.

William Savage

On the Preparation of Printing Ink; both Black and Coloured
1832. pp. 13-20

Introductory Observations on Printing Ink.

Printing Ink of a rich and durable tone, and of a superior quality, is so essential to the appearance of an elegant book, that it is impossible for any Printer to produce a splendid work, even with all the skill and improved knowledge of the present times, except he be provided with such an article.

The want of this superior article has been severely felt by numerous Printers who aspired to rank with the few who had obtained pre-eminence in this art; but they invariably failed in their endeavours, although in their profession possessed of skill, the best materials, and an anxious desire to rival the beautiful productions which issued from the presses of Bensley and of Bulmer, of Davison, Whittingham, &c.

The real grievance was, that there was not any good Printing Ink to be purchased; and after procuring the best that could be obtained, and bestowing the utmost care and skill upon their work, and making it look of a very superior character when first printed, they had the mortification to find, after a few months had elapsed, that the Ink turned brown, the edges of the letters and the back of the page were stained yellow, owing to the oil in the Ink having separated from the colouring matter, and that it thus disfigured the paper, and destroyed the beauty of their work and of the book; while the productions of those few who had raised themselves to eminence in the art remained unchanged, preserving all their pristine beauty.

The principal cause of this eminence was the superior quality of the Ink they used, which they prepared themselves, and kept the method of so doing a profound secret, which they guarded with the utmost care and strictness, and thus preserved the monopoly of fine printing in their own hands.

At the time that I am speaking of, the production of Macklin's Bible, Bowyer's History of England, and Boydell's Shakspeare—which were exertions to rival and excel the famed typographical works of Bodoni at Parma, and Didot at Paris—so greatly surpassed any thing that had previously proceeded from the English press, as to have induced a great spirit of emulation to improve printing generally in England, which then consisted of two kinds only—the commonest and the finest that could be produced. Other causes also combined to strengthen this spirit; namely, the increased diffusion of knowledge by the institution of Sunday Schools, and the introduction of Bell's and of Lancaster's systems of education, which increased the number of readers, increased the demand for books, increased the number of printers to meet that demand, and consequently increased that emulation to enable them to enter into competition with those who had obtained a great name in the art. Another cause also operated to produce an improvement in printing—the Act of the thirty-ninth of George the Third, Chapter seventy-nine, for the Suppression of Seditious Societies, obliged every printer to affix his name and address to what he printed; thus those who exerted themselves to produce neat work came conspicuously before the public, while it stimulated the slovenly and careless to exert themselves in order to preserve their business, and equal their active competitors.

But, as I have previously observed, the want of good Printing Ink was a serious drawback on these exertions towards a general improvement of the art of printing; for although the few Ink makers by profession endeavoured to improve the article, yet either from a want of knowledge of the qualities that were required, or of the properties of the ingredients or the process of compounding them, or of all these qualifications together, it is an undoubted fact that their improvements did not equal nor even keep pace with the skill of the printer in his manipulations. I have been continually for many years in the habit of looking at printing at the press side, which has appeared of a superior quality; but when I have examined the same sheets after a lapse of one or two years, the beauty of the printing had disappeared; the Ink had acquired a brown colour, and the paper, to the size of the printed page, by reason of the oil being imperfectly prepared, was stained of a dirty yellowish brown colour, and thus all the skill, expence, and care, bestowed on the workmanship were rendered of no avail.

Yet it would be unfair to the manufacturers of Printing Ink to assert that no improvement in the article has taken place; for as their number increased, it caused competition and excited a spirit of emulation among them, that has certainly been the means of improving the Ink of commerce;

but still, as I have just observed, it has not kept pace with the general improvement in the art of printing.

Even the limited knowledge that is possessed by the very few manufacturers of this article of the properties required in its composition, is carefully guarded as a profound secret; so that the printer who may be desirous of having Ink of a very superior quality is not able to form it de novo, for want of information on the subject, but is obliged to take the Ink of commerce as a foundation to work upon, and improve that which he thus tacitly acknowledges is of an inferior quality, and to attempt to change that which is bad inherently to excellence:—the thing is impracticable.

It is my intention, in the following pages, to endeavour to supply this desideratum in the art of printing, for, except in my work on Decorative Printing, there are no directions published by which Ink can be made which the workmen of the present day could use, on account of the despatch that is required. The Ink made by any of these directions would invariably clog up the type in a few impressions, and the form would have to be brushed over with lie repeatedly, and washed and dried, to the great delay of business and loss to the workmen, independently of the very inferior article that would be produced in the quality of the printing, and with machines it would be impossible to use it: the receipt which I published was for a very superior and expensive Ink, that would not be suitable for the general run of business.

I shall insert all the receipts that have been published in respectable works, and which have been repeatedly quoted and praised, with some observations on each of them, to show in what they fail;—this I am induced to do that the reader may have before him all that has been written on the subject by men of abilities,—and then add the result of my own labours, which is derived from long-continued numerous experiments and practical experience.

Nicholson, a man of science, and of great research in the processes of arts and manufactures, in his "Dictionary of

Chemistry," when treating on this subject says, "the particulars of the process by which Ink of the best quality is made are kept secret by the few manufacturers of this article. It is probable, that the demand is not sufficient to afford inducements for men of research to make many experiments on this subject, and it is not unlikely that much may depend on minute circumstances in the management."

To me it appears that all the directions which have been published had one origin, and that they have been given with some slight variations uninterruptedly from the latter part of the seventeenth century; for the first that I can trace were given by Moxon, in his "Mechanick Exercises," in 1677, as the method practised by the Dutch in making Ink, which he praises highly as being much superior to the English method; but whoever looks at the productions of the press at that period, when the art was at its lowest state, and compares them with those of the present day, will immediately perceive that the ink then used would not answer now, even for its appearance, without taking into consideration the foulness of its working.

From the superior description of Works entrusted to me to print, I was obliged, in order to equal the productions of our best printers, to turn my attention seriously to this subject in the year 1808; and I then found, from repeated disappointments, that it required a printer, who knew from practical experience what properties were required in Ink, to make a real improvement on the article of commerce: and when I was engaged on my work on Decorative Printing, I was still further obliged to pursue my object by dint of experiments in coloured Inks, for there existed no precedents to guide me; and I feel a high gratification in perceiving the great improvement that has taken place in ornamental printing since the publication of that book.

The information which I am now throwing open to the Public is the result of twenty-three years of application devoted to this peculiar subject. I have pursued my object with ardour, because I saw in it capabilities which I believed I saw alone. Wonderful and extensive as is the power of the printing press in diffusing knowledge over the globe, I saw and felt that it had yet a capability untried and unacknowledged of producing works that might deservedly raise its claims to rank among the Fine Arts. I have had the satisfaction of realizing my expectations: I have shown in my work on Decorative Printing how successfully drawings may be imitated by means of the common printing press, to the surprise of all who could estimate the difficulties attendant on such an undertaking, towards which no precedent information existed, and wherein every advance was made by dint of experiment.

William Savage

Dictionary of the Art of Printing

1841. pp. 177-181

Composing.

The term composing includes the practical knowledge of picking up letters, spacing, justifying lines, and emptying the composing stick when full.

Although expedition is a most desirable qualification in a compositor, yet alone it is far from constituting a good workman: and the man who possesses no other claims to the title will be found competent to little more than setting reprints, in which no judgment is required, and where he has only to arrange letter for letter, point for point, and line for line; on which employment he may whistle, sing, talk, or laugh, without inconvenience to himself; for the process being merely mechanical, and the mind not being occupied in the smallest degree, if he make a mistake of a word, it will be detected at the end of the line; or, if there be a double, or an out, of lines, either will be detected when the page is finished.

How different is the case with the man who is anxious to deserve the title of a good workman, and to maintain it: in his youth he has been equally desirous with the other to acquire expedition; and, having attained it, he has felt that other requisites were necessary;—he has read, to obtain information—he has examined the best workmanship, as specimens for his guidance—he endeavours to compose accurately—he is careful and uniform in his spacing—he justifies his lines to an equal tightness—he divides his words, when necessary to divide them, correctly, and with a regard to appearance—and when occasional bits of rule work occur, they are marked by a degree of neatness in being cut to precise lengths, and in the corners fitting with precision—in all the work that passes through his hands there appear the marks of attention and skill.

When a master printer undertakes a work which requires more than ordinary care, and is difficult to execute, the superiority of the man who has endeavoured to improve himself is evident: he is selected to perform it; and he then feels the advantage of his perseverance. At work upon a difficult subject, with an ill written manuscript, his first proofs show him equal to the task—his arrangements of the matter are judicious—his punctuation is correct—when particular sorts are to be justified, they are done with accuracy—when an accented letter is required that cannot be procured in a single type, he makes it with neatness—and when his proof returns from the reader, he will frequently correct it in as little time, as a slovenly compositor will require to correct a proof of a similar size, that is a reprint.

The results to the slovenly and the good compositor are

very different. The first is only employed during a flush of work; when that ceases, he has to seek fresh employment; perhaps does not meet with any for some weeks; again obtains a temporary engagement; and thus continues, till old age approaches, and he is rendered incapable of working. The good work-man, on the contrary, is prized by his employer, especially if the latter be a workman himself, and a man of judgment. He is looked up to by his fellow-workmen; his situation is permanent, if he choose; his abilities qualify him to be a reader, and if his mind lead him that way, he may obtain such a situation. His knowledge and his merit fit him to become the overseer of a large house; where he has many advantages, and where he continues with credit to himself: unless, perhaps, he chooses to commence business on his own account, which is frequently done, when he invariably obtains the countenance and support of those who have witnessed his skill, his knowledge, his attention, and his industry.

There is another class of compositors who neither possess much skill; nor are very expeditious: I mean such as are of a sober, steady habit. These are useful men in an office where there is a number of reprints; they go on from year to year in a regular routine, and never step out of it: the employer can always depend on them for a regular amount of work, if they have sufficient employment.

There are too many, both good and bad workmen, who lose their time in drinking, gaming, and other vicious and idle pursuits: such persons pay doubly for their dissipation, for they squander the fruits of their earnings, and cut off the source of supply, by neglecting their employment. These men will never be employed in any respectable printing office, where they are known, except on a temporary engagement in a case of emergency. They introduce strife and discord wherever they are, and frequently lead astray the inexperienced youth: they disregard equally instruction and advice, and are not awakened to a sense of their condition, till the most severe lessons in this world are unitedly experienced—old age, poverty, and contempt.

The mere art of picking up letters, and arranging them in the composing stick, is looked upon by many compositors as constituting the whole of their business; who in consequence think that if they can succeed in picking letters up with facility, they become first-rate workmen; and the terms "Swifts," and "Fire Eaters," by which expeditious compositors are designated in a printing office, gratify their vanity.

It is not necessary to give specific rules, and a minute description, of the manner of picking up each letter, because it is impossible for them to hold good, the letters lying in every possible direction. A few general rules may suffice—to take up the letter at that end where the face is—if the nick be not upwards, to turn it upwards in its progress to the composing stick—to convey it to the line in the composing stick with as few motions as possible—to aim at no flourishes with the hand, which only lose time.

I would advise an inexperienced youth, when he comes to work among a number of men, to observe the manner of one of the best and quickest compositors: he will, perhaps, at first conclude that he is looking at a very slow workman, for the first appearance is fallacious; but when he examines more closely he will find his mistake, for what he at first took for slowness is the true principle of expedition; he will perceive no false motion, which invariably delays progress; the fingers go to one particular letter, take it up, convey it to the line direct, while the eye is directed to another letter which the fingers convey in the same manner to the line; thus letter after letter accumulate to words, lines, and pages, with a quickness that looks like magic, while to the spectator it seems to be only the pace of the tortoise. Let him look at another; there appears all bustle, all expedition; the body and head in continual motion; the hand so quick in its evolutions, that he gazes with astonishment on the apparent rapidity of arranging the letters: let him look again with more attention, and he will find that the man whom he supposed so slow makes no mistake, loses not time, but continues steadily and uniformly making progress: while the other frequently misses taking hold of his letter; then makes two or three flourishes with his hand and his head before he takes hold of another; and then his hand continues dancing and see-sawing, and after three or four of such motions, made with great rapidity, the letter is finally deposited in the line. This manner of lifting the letters is in reality the pace of the tortoise, although it has the appearance of the speed of the hare.

Regularity of spacing, and a due proportion of distance between words, contribute in a material degree to improve the appearance of a book.

When the lines are very short, or the type very large in proportion to their length, all general rules, both of dividing and spacing, must give way to necessity; for in such cases it is impossible at all times to space regularly, or to divide the words correctly.

There is a great diversity of opinion with respect to spacing; some authors and printers choosing to have the words wide apart, and others, on the contrary, preferring to have them nearly close together; the one, requiring an en quadrat, or two thick spaces, and the other, a thin space only, between the words. Both of these, in my opinion, go to an extreme: I prefer using a thick space generally, and justifying with thinner and hair spaces; so that there will rarely be a necessity for any violent inequality in the distance of the words from each other.

When a work is double leaded, or has reglet between the lines, it requires to be wider spaced than when it is solid: in the first two cases, two middling spaces, or a thick and a thin space, will not be too much; in the latter, a thick space will be quite sufficient. And it is necessary to attend to these circumstances; for printing that is open does not harmonize when close spaced, any more than solid matter does when wide spaced, which makes it look full of pigeon holes; for the distance between the words should bear some proportion to the distance between the lines.

When one or two letters require to be got in, or to be driven out, the difference between a thick space and a middling one is not perceptible to the eye, particularly if the compositor is careful to place the latter before or after a v or w, after a comma that comes before a v or w, or after a y; and, in like manner an additional hair space will not be perceptible if it come after an f, or before a j: or if it come between db, dh, dk, dl, lb, lh, lk, or ll.

The most expeditious mode of regular spacing, perhaps, is to take the spaces as they rise; for there being in the box only three sorts, the thin and the hair spaces being in separate boxes, there will not be any violent disproportion if the line should be full at the first; and the slight disproportion may be easily remedied by changing the situation of two or three; if the line should not be quite full, then the introduction of a few thin spaces will equalise the distances; or the substitution of a few thick spaces for middling ones will have the same effect.

In setting a line of capitals, a careful workman will pay attention to the bearing off of different letters, for many of them when they fall together stand as if there were a space between them, and produce a bad effect; to remedy this inequality, hair spaces, or bits of paper, are required between those letters that stand close. The inequality is still greater in many instances in a line of Italic capitals, and of course requires the same remedy.

It would be desirable, and would tend to facilitate regular spacing, if there were a greater number of hair spaces cast to a fount than is now the case.

In poetry, the size of the type and the measure are usually so arranged as to admit the longest line to come into the measure, without having occasion to turn it: an opportunity is thus allowed for regular spacing, which is generally done with thick spaces. When a work in poetry is commenced, it is usual for the compositor to divide his space box up the middle with a piece of reglet, or with a piece of thin wood, made to fit tight, and to assort his thick spaces on one side, and the thinner on the other, to save time and trouble in picking them out.

As the measure for poetry is sometimes made as narrow as will conveniently allow the regular lines to come in, both to save quadrats, and also to lessen the price of composing, it not unfrequently happens that a line containing long syllables will not admit of thick spaces; in this case, the usual practice is to space close, and get in the line if possible, even with hair spaces, for turning it is attended with inconveniences; the page must be made up short, or long, to preserve the couplets, and it affects the next page, in preventing the stanzas backing each other.

A compositor will always find it advantageous to justify his lines to an equal tightness; and of this he must be sensible when he has to lock up his form: if he have been careless in this instance he will experience a loss of time and find a difficulty in getting his form to lift; and when it does lift, by means of sticking his bodkin into quadrats and spaces to tighten those lines that are slack, it will never be safe; for it is more than probable that many letters will draw out at press, and cause errors in that sheet, (for pressmen are generally careless how they replace a letter that has drawn, and, when it is discovered, they are satisfied if they put it into the right word,) the pressmen scold the compositor, who also, if he be working in a companionship, and should not be the last in the sheet, gets scolded by the compositor who has to lock up the forms, for his carelessness, and for the additional trouble which it causes.

I would avoid having a lower case f at the end of a line; for, being a kerned letter, the dot at the end of the curve is almost sure to be broken off while the sheet is being worked at press.

It is not possible to give particular rules for justifying all the sorts that occur in many works, and that are not in a printing office:—for a Ç it will be necessary to cut away the shank to the bottom of the face of the letter, and justify a figure of 5 with the top back dash cut off; a long m̄, n̄, or any other letter, must be cut away to the upper part of the letter, and a small lower case l, with the fine lines cut away, fixed flat above; a short y̆ may be made by taking the bottom of an o; m̊ and ñ by cutting the front of a small a away, and laying it lengthways; ŵ and ŷ by inverting a lower case v, after cutting away the cross lines, and making the thick line equal to the fine one with a sharp knife.

Cutting away the shank allows the additional part to stand close to the face of the letter, which improves the appearance. In some instances it will be necessary to cut part of a lead away above the letter, and justify the addition in the vacancy. The compositor should, by all means, be careful to justify every sort that is added so tight as to prevent it from drawing out at press; but not so tight, as to force the words above and below out of line; in fact, they ought to be so managed as, when justified to the letter, to form unitedly its regular body in depth when it is practicable. The compositor should also be careful to proportion the size of the accent or mark to be justified to the size of the letter, that there may be no disproportion between them.

I would recommend to every compositor when he goes to a fresh house, where it is likely he may work some time, to ascertain what founts are in the house, with the two line letters, blacks, flowers, &c.: this knowledge will give him facilities, and enable him to compose a title, or a job, with less sacrifice of time, than if he were not acquainted with the materials contained in the office.

T. H. Fielding

The Art of Engraving

1841. pp. 29-38

Line Engraving.

Of all the various kinds of engraving, the art we are about to describe stands pre-eminently the first. However it may be surpassed by other branches of the profession in the representation of certain objects, yet as a whole it is decidedly superior to the rest. It cannot produce the velvety softness, intense depth, and harmonious mingling of light and shade, which is given by mezzotint. Neither can it, even when aided by the ruling machine, produce that silvery clearness, or deep transparent tone perceived in aquatint; not like it, reproduce the *dragging, scumbling*, and accidental touches of the artist's brush. In crispness and brilliancy it is far exceeded by wood engraving. Still it stands before all others, and we cannot but see with regret, though not surprise, its present declining state.

When steel was first applied to line engraving, the immense number of impressions it was found capable of producing, enabled the publishers to offer to the world, works beautifully illustrated, at a much cheaper rate than had hitherto been done. A new class of publications, we mean the annuals, were introduced as a vehicle for spreading more rapidly the impressions from steel plates, and the most beautiful productions of our best engravers were flung with a prodigal hand before the public, at a price for which they ought never to have been sold, and which only an excessive sale could render profitable. We are no enemies to cheapness in any thing, and still less in whatever may contribute to the mental enjoyment of the public, but when that cheapness is obtained by the reduced income of the artist, reduced, not from extravagant gains to fair remuneration, but from fair remuneration to insufficiency; when such is the case we cannot but lament, whilst we admire the beautiful works which fill our portfolio, the sacrifice by which they have been so cheaply obtained.

The cause of this deterioration was simply the excessive sale of these illustrated works, which created a demand for line engravers far beyond what the population of England, rich as she is, ought to support. But the fashion for annuals, like all other fashions, passed away. One by one they sunk into oblivion, and left the artists they had helped to create, to seek an existence in other countries, or by attempting some other branch of the profession. The public, weary with seeing in every shop and on every table the beautiful engravings which steel plates had showered upon the land, like a child surfeited with sweets, was glad to turn to something else, and mezzotint became the fashion. Then it was that the reduced sale of illustrated works, no longer allowed the publishers to offer a fair remuneration, and the quantity of engravers unemployed were forced to accept the little they could afford to give.

Such are the causes of the present depressed state of the art, and were these all the evils arising from engraving on steel, if it were merely a stagnation arising from too great a production, however much we might regret the losses which line engravers must for a while sustain, still we know that a few years must bring back the art to a more healthy state. But when the hardness of the metal was found to admit of finer work, then came in fashion the excessively finished style of the present day, which, whilst it increases the mechanical difficulties, tends to reduce all engravers to the same level, or what is still worse, allows some whose only merit consists in a capability of laying lines closer than others, to usurp the place of real talent. This is indeed an evil, and we are afraid that many years must pass away before the vitiated taste of the public can bear the works of real genius, unfettered by the microscopic finish of the present style.

The process of line engraving consists at present, in first etching the plate, and then after it is bitten in, finishing it with the graver and dry point. Formerly, however, it was the custom to begin and finish a plate with the graver only; but this method has long been laid aside, as the use of the etching needle gives so much greater freedom in the representation of almost every object.

Of the method of laying the ground, transferring the subject to the plate by means of tracing, and of sharpening the graver, needle, &c., we have already spoken under the head of etching. The manner of handling the needle is, however very different, as in all the flat tints a ruler is made use of. Clear blue skies are done by means of the ruling machine, of which the following is a description. "On a straight bar of steel is placed a socket, which slides backwards and forwards with a steady, but even motion. To the side of the socket is fitted a perpendicular tube, which receives a steel wire or any other hard substance, called a pen. This pen has a point like an etching needle, and is pressed down by the action of a spring. If, then, a copper plate covered with the etching-ground is placed under the ruler, which should be supported at each end, and raised about an inch above it, the point of the pen may be caused to reach it; and if the socket to which the pen is attached be drawn along the bar, it will form a straight line upon the plate, more even, but in other respects the same as if that line had been drawn by hand with a ruler. Now, if the plate or the ruler be moved, backwards or forwards, in a direction parallel to this first line, any number of lines may be drawn in the same manner."

In the machine, therefore, a very exact screw, acting upon a box confined by a slide and connected with the bar or board upon which the plate rests, produces the requisite motion; and a contrivance or index is used to measure the exact portion of a turn required before any stroke is drawn. Such is the principle of the machine most generally used; but the point or pen employed should not be made of steel, which however well tempered will require frequent sharpening, and must therefore inevitably draw strokes deficient in perfect uniformity. The pen should have a diamond point, which when once properly figured, remains constantly the same, and imparts an admirable degree of regularity and sweetness to the work.

Though the ruler is used in laying flat tints, it does not follow that the lines made with it are to be straight; on the contrary, they are made to take the form most suited to the object by slightly moving the hand, taking care to make them parallel. But the greatest difficulty, and what requires the longest practice to attain, is to give that equal pressure to the needle, so that every line may be the same depth, width, and distance from each other, without which it is entirely hopeless to obtain an even tint. This capability of laying flat tints, and of ruling parallel lines excessively close without running into each other, is so essential, that no one can expect to make a decent plate till he has fully accomplished it; and the first business of the learner should be by continual practice to obtain a readiness and certainty in the management of the ruler and needle. He must also be equally capable of laying parallel lines of the same strength without the aid of the ruler, and must seek to acquire a freedom of handling in etching grass and the foliage of trees in landscape, and the flowing lines required in drapery and the waves of the sea.

In etching a plate to be finished as a line engraving, every part which is white, such as white drapery, satin, light water, ice, white clouds, the white fur of animals except when in shade, and the light parts of flesh, &c., ought to be left untouched by the aquafortis, and laid in with the dry-point or graver.

The following extracts from a celebrated work on Engraving, aided by the examination of the prints of the best professors of the art, will be found worthy of attention. "The strokes of the graver should never be crossed too much in the lozenge manner, particularly in the representation of flesh, because sharp angles produce the unpleasing effect of lattice work, and take from the eye the repose which is agreeable to it in all kinds of picturesque designs; we should except the case of clouds, tempests, waves of the sea, the skins of hairy animals, or the leaves of trees, where this method of crossing may be admitted. But in avoiding the lozenge it is not proper to get entirely into the square, which would give too much of the hardness of stone. In conducting the strokes, the action of the figures and of all their parts should be considered, and it should be observed how they advance towards, or recede from the eye, and the graver should be guided according to the risings or cavities of the muscles or folds, making the strokes wider and fainter in the lights, and closer and firmer in the shades. Thus the figures will not appear jagged, and the hand should be lightened in such a manner, that the outlines may be formed and terminated without being cut too hard; however, though the strokes break off where the muscle begins, yet they ought always to have a certain connection with each other, so that the first stroke may often serve by its return to make the second, which will show the freedom of the engraver.

In engraving the flesh, the effect may be produced, in the lighter parts and middle tints, by long pecks of the graver, rather than by light lines or by round dots, or by dots a little lengthened by the graver, or, best of all, by a judicious mixture of these together.

In engraving the hair and the beard, the engraver should begin his work by laying the principal grounds and sketching the chief shades in a careless manner, or with a few strokes, and he may finish it at leisure with finer and thinner strokes at the extremities. When architecture is to be represented, except it be old and ruinous buildings, the work ought not to be made very black, because as edifices are commonly constructed either of stone or white marble, the colour being reflected on all sides does not produce dark shades as in other substances. When sculpture is to be represented, white points must not be put in the pupils of the eyes of figures as in engravings after paintings, nor must the hair or beard be represented as in nature, which makes the locks appear flowing in the air, because in sculpture there can be no such appearance.

In engraving cloths of different kinds, linen should be done with finer and closer lines than other sorts, and be executed with single strokes. Woollen cloth should be engraved wide in proportion to the coarseness or fineness of the stuff, and when the strokes are crossed, the second should be smaller than the first, and the third than the second. Shining stuffs, which are generally of silk or satin, and which produce flat and broken folds, should be engraved more hard and more straight than others, with one or two strokes as their colours are bright or otherwise; and between the first course of lines other smaller must be occasionally introduced, which is called interlining. Velvet and plush are expressed in the same manner, and should always be interlined. Metals, as armour, &c., are also represented by interlining, or by clear single strokes. In architecture, the strokes which form the rounding of objects should tend to the point of sight, and when whole columns occur, it is proper to produce the effect as much as possible by perpendicular strokes. If a cross stroke is put, it should be at right angles, and wider and thinner than the first stroke. The strokes ought to be frequently discontinued and broken for sharp and craggy objects. Objects that are distant, towards the horizon should be kept very tender. Waters that are calm and still, are best represented by strokes that are straight and parallel to the horizon, interlined with those that are finer, omitting such places as in consequence of gleams of light exhibit the shining appearance of water; and the forms of objects reflected upon the water at a small distance from it, or on the banks of the water, are expressed by the same strokes retouched more strongly or faintly as occasion may require, and even by some that are perpendicular. For agitated waters, as the waves of the sea, the first strokes should follow the figure of the waves, and may be interlined, and the cross strokes ought to be very lozenge. In cascades, the strokes should follow the fall and be interlined. In engraving clouds, the engraver or needle should sport where they appear thick and agitated, in turning every way according to their form and their agitation. If the clouds are dark so that two strokes are necessary, they should be crossed more lozenge than the figures, and the second strokes should be rather wider than the first. The flat clouds that are lost insensibly in the clear sky should be made by strokes parallel to the horizon, and a little waving; if second strokes are required, they should be more or less lozenge, and when they are brought to the extremity the land should be so lightened that they may form no outline. The flat and clear sky is represented by parallel and straight strokes, without the least turning. In landscapes, the trees, rocks, earth, herbage, and indeed every part except white objects, should be etched as much as possible; nothing should be left for the graver, but perfecting, softening, and strengthening."

The above observations will be found very useful to refer to, though perhaps after all, the examination of the prints of the best engravers will be found the best instruction that the beginner can have; but then that examination ought to be, not merely to see how certain work is performed, but the manner of executing the representation of the same object by different engravers should be carefully observed, and that which is best selected as a model, remarking at the same time wherein consists its excellence, and in what manner it differs from the rest.

Alois Senefelder

A Complete Course of Lithography

1819. pp. 9-11, 203-205, 256-258

As I come now in my narrative to that period, from which the Art of Lithography may be said to have drawn its direct origin, I hope I may crave the indulgence of the reader, if I mention even the most trifling circumstances, to which the new art was indebted for its existence.

I had just succeeded in my little laboratory in polishing a stone plate, which I intended to cover with etching ground, in order to continue my exercises in writing backwards, when my mother entered the room, and desired me to write her a bill for the washer-woman, who was waiting for the linen; I happened not to have even the smallest slip of paper at hand, as my little stock of paper had been entirely exhausted by taking proof impressions from the stones; nor was there even a drop of ink in the inkstand. As the matter would not admit of delay, and we had nobody in the house to send for a supply of the deficient materials, I resolved to write the list with my ink prepared with wax, soap, and lampblack, on the stone which I had just polished, and from which I could copy it at leisure.

Some time after this I was just going to wipe this writing from the stone, when the idea all at once struck me, to try what would be the effect of such a writing with my prepared ink, if I were to bite in the stone with aqua-fortis; and whether, perhaps, it might not be possible to apply printing ink to it, in the same way as to wood engravings, and so take impressions from it. I immediately hastened to put this idea in execution, surrounded the stone with a border of wax, and covered the surface of the stone, to the height of two inches, with a mixture of one part of aqua-fortis, and ten parts of

water, which I left standing five minutes on it; and on examin-
ing the effect of this experiment, I found the writing, elevated
about a 10th part of a line, (or 1-120th part of an inch.)
Some of the finer, and not sufficiently distinct, lines, had
suffered in some measure, but the greater part of the letters
had not been damaged at all in their breadth, considering
their *elevation*; so that I confidently hoped to obtain very
clear impressions, chiefly from printed characters, in which
there are not many fine strokes.

I now proceeded to apply the printing ink to the stone, for
which purpose I first used a common printer's ball; but, after
some unsuccessful trials, I found that a thin piece of board,
covered with fine cloth, answered the purpose perfectly, and
communicated the ink in a more equal manner, than any
other material I had before used. My farther trials of this
method greatly encouraged my perseverance. The application of the printing ink was easier than in the other
methods, and I could take impressions with a fourth part of
the power that was requisite for an engraving so that the
stones were not at all liable to the danger of breaking; and,
what was of the greatest moment to me, this method of
printing was an entirely new invention, which had occurred
to nobody before me. I could, therefore, hope to obtain a
patent for it, or even some assistance from the government,
which, in similar instances, had shown the greatest liberality
in encouraging and promoting new inventions, which I
thought of less importance.

Thus the new art was invented, and I lost no time in
making myself a perfect master of it; but, in order to exercise
it so as to gain a livelihood by it, a little capital was indispensable to construct a press, purchase stones, paper, and other
utensils. But as I could not afford even this trifling expense, I
saw myself again on the point of being obliged to relinquish
all my fond hopes and prospects of success, unless I could
devise an expedient to obtain the necessary money. At length
I hit upon one, which was to enlist as a private in the artillery,

as a substitute for a friend of mine, who promised me a premium of 200 florins. This sum I thought would be sufficient to establish my first press, to which I intended to devote all my leisure, and the produce of which, I hoped, would soon enable me to procure my discharge from the army; besides my knowledge of mathematics, mechanics, and fortification, might possibly promote my views in this new career.

The Pen, or Hair-Brush, Drawing.

This is one of the principal manners of Lithography; and, perhaps, the most popular of all; as it is applicable to many purposes of common life. It not only imitates all sorts of writing and printing, and in many cases even surpasses them in elegance, but it is also applicable to all drawings where the nicety of a well executed copper-plate is not required. The expedition of the execution, and the short space of time in which a number of impressions can be produced, highly recommend it. It requires but little penetration to foresee that, at some future time, when more attention shall be paid to it by experienced and clever artists, it will be used for the higher productions of art.

But advantageous as this manner is, it has hitherto been only used for writing and music; and it is difficult to persuade people of its excellent qualities. A circumstance, apparently trifling, is the cause of the small success of this manner with artists. I have met with but two persons who, from the very first day of their study, could reconcile themselves to the use of the steel pens, used for drawing on the stone, and were able to write with them; these were my brother Clement, and a gentleman of the name of Börner; all other artists, without exception, had more or less to struggle with difficulties, which generally exhausted their zeal and patience at the end of a few days. In another part of this work, I have already explained the manner of producing these pens; and I shall, therefore, proceed immediately to the description of the manipulation of this manner. Here it is not necessary to be very nice in the selection of a stone, for even stones of a less perfect description may be used for it without risk. The harder and finer, however, a stone is, the better it is for it. If the stones have previously been used for other drawings, it is necessary to rub them down till all vestiges of the former drawing disappear. It is immaterial what substance is used in rubbing down the stone, provided it becomes perfectly smooth, so that the pen meet with no impediment in drawing or writing upon it. In order, however, to produce clear lines on the stone, a farther preparation is necessary, by which the spreading of the ink on the surface is effectually prevented. One part of weak oil, dissolved in three parts of spirits of turpentine, forms a mixture, with which the well polished and well dried surface of the stone ought to be washed; the stone ought then, as quickly afterwards as possible, to be carefully wiped with clean linen; or blotting paper, so that only a very thin coat of the mixture may remain on it, and it will then be rendered easily accessible to the aqua-fortis. This must be done some hours before beginning to draw, partly in order to avoid the strong and disagreeable smell of the turpentine, and partly because immediately after washing the stone it does not receive the ink from the pen so well as it does afterwards. Time does not annihilate the effect of this preparation, and it may even take place some months before using the stone; which, in this case, requires only to be well cleaned from dust by a brush, a precaution that must be repeated several times during the day, while at work on it, otherwise dust will get into the pen.

A drawing on paper transferred on stone.

Transfer and Tracing Manner.

In Pen, or Chalk drawings, all the lines and points which are to take ink and be printed, are drawn with a greasy matter on the stone itself. But there is another manner in Lithography where the drawing or writing with the same unctuous composition is made on paper, and is transferred from thence by artificial dissolution to the stone, and printed from it. This manner is peculiar to the chemical printing, and I am strongly inclined to believe, that it is the principal and most important part of my discovery. In order to multiply copies of your ideas by printing, it is no longer necessary to learn to write in an inverted sense; but every person who with common ink can write on paper, may do the same with chemical ink, and by the transfer of his writing to the stone, it can be multiplied *ad infinitum*. At Munich, at Paris, and St. Petersburgh, this manner is already used in the government offices. All resolutions, edicts, orders, &c., agreed to in the cabinet meetings, are written down on paper by the secretary with chemical ink; in the space of an hour fifty impressions may be had and distributed at pleasure. For circulars, and in general all such orders of government as must be rapidly distributed, an invention like this is of the utmost consequence; and I am convinced, that before ten years shall elapse, all the European governments will be possessed of a lithographical establishment for transferring writing to the stone. In time of war, this method is of the greatest use for the general staff of the army; it supplies entirely the want of a field printing-office, and admits of greater despatch and secrecy. The commanding officer may write his orders with his own hand, and in his presence a number of impressions may be taken from them by a person who can neither write nor read; or by placing the stone in such a manner that the reverse is turned towards the printer, he may be prevented from reading any thing. If plans of military positions or topographical sketches must be given, the engineer has only to draw them on paper, and in a short space of time all the general officers may be supplied with them. In commerce and trade the transfer manner will, ere long, be generally introduced; especially in great commercial houses, where it often happens that a quick and accurate multiplication of price lists, letters, and accounts is of the utmost importance. Men of letters and authors may by means of it multiply in a cheap and easy manner their manuscripts, which they are often obliged to transcribe with great pain and trouble to themselves. Music printing will, by the introduction of this manner, receive new life, as the expenses of engraving will be very greatly reduced. In all countries, where type-printing is not yet introduced and type foundries are unknown, the transfer-manner will obtain the preference; and even in European printing-offices, where a number of books in the oriental languages are printed, in those of the Bible societies for instance, it will be found highly advantageous.—It will be of the utmost benefit to artists by enabling them to obtain fac similes of their drawings. From the most sincere conviction of its utility, and not any motive of vanity, I have thus detailed in a brief manner the various advantages of transfer-printing; it would indeed be an easy matter, by expatiating on these advantages, to fill a whole book. I wish from the bottom of my heart to gain friends to this manner, and to point out the various important purposes to which it may be applied, in order that clever artists may devote themselves to its improvement.

John Jackson and W. A. Chatto

A Treatise on Wood Engraving
(1839). 1861. pp. 572-575, 589-591, 602, 603

Before proceeding to engrave a delicate pencil drawing the block ought to be covered with paper, with the exception of the part on which it is intended to begin. Soft paper ought not to be used for this purpose, as such is most likely to partially efface the drawing when the hand is pressed upon

A TREATISE

ON

WOOD ENGRAVING

Historical and Practical

WITH UPWARDS OF THREE HUNDRED ILLUSTRATIONS
ENGRAVED ON WOOD

BY JOHN JACKSON.

THE HISTORICAL PORTION BY W. A. CHATTO.

Second Edition

WITH A NEW CHAPTER ON THE ARTISTS OF THE PRESENT DAY

BY HENRY G. BOHN

AND 145 ADDITIONAL WOOD ENGRAVINGS.

LONDON
HENRY G. BOHN, YORK STREET, COVENT GARDEN.
M. DCCC. LXI.

the block. Moderately stout post-paper with a glazed surface is the best; though some engravers, in order to preserve their eyes, which become affected by white paper, cover the block with blue paper, which is usually too soft, and thus expose the drawing to injury. The dingey, grey, and over-done appearance of several modern wood-cuts is doubtless owing, in a great measure, to the block when in course of engraving having been covered with soft paper, which has partially effaced the drawing. The drawing, which originally may have been clear and *touchy*, loses its brightness, and becomes indistinct from its frequent contact with the soft pliable paper; the spirited dark touches which give it effect are rubbed down to a sober grey, and all the other parts, from the same cause, are comparatively weak. The cut, being engraved according to the appearance of the drawing, is tame, flat, and spiritless.

Different engravers have different methods of fastening the paper to the block. Some fix it with gum, or with wafers at the sides; but this is not a good mode, for as often as it is necessary to take a view of the whole block, in order to judge of the progress of the work, the paper must be torn off, and afterwards replaced by means of new wafers or fresh gum, so that before the cut is finished the sides of the block are covered with bits of paper in the manner of a wall or shop-front covered with fragments of posting-bills. The most convenient mode of fastening the paper is to first wrap a piece of stiff and stout thread three or four times round the edges of the block, and then after making the end fast to remove it. The paper is then to be closely fitted to the block, and the edges being brought over the sides, the 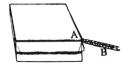 thread is to be re-placed above it. If the turns of the thread be too tight to pass over the last corner of the block, A, a piece string, B, being passed within them and firmly pulled, in the manner here represented, will cause them to stretch a little and pass over on to the edge without difficulty. When this plan is adopted the paper forms a kind of moveable cap, which can be taken off at pleasure to view the progress of the work, and replaced without the least trouble.

I have long been of opinion that many young persons, when beginning to learn the art of wood engraving, have injured their sight by unnecessarily using a magnifying glass. At the very commencement of their pupilage boys will furnish themselves with a glass of this kind, as if it were as much a matter of course as a set of gravers; they sometimes see men use a glass, and as at this period they are prone to ape their elders in the profession, *they* must have one also; and as they generally choose such as magnify most, the result not unfrequently is that their sight is considerably impaired before they are capable of executing anything that really requires much nicety of vision.

I would recommend all persons to avoid the use of glasses of any kind, whether single magnifiers or spectacles, until impaired sight renders such aids necessary; and even then to commence with such as are of small magnifying power. The habit of viewing minute objects alternately with a magnifying glass and the naked eye—applying the glass every two or three minutes—is, I am satisfied, injurious to the sight. The magnifying glass used by wood engravers is similar to that used by watch-makers, and consists of a single lens, fitted into a short tube, which is rather wider at the end applied to the eye. As the glass seldom can be fixed so firmly to the eye as to entirely dispense with holding it, the engraver is thus frequently obliged to apply his left hand to keep it in its place; as he cannot hold the block with the same hand at the same time, or move it as may be required, so as to enable him to execute his work with freedom, the consequence is, that the engraving of a person who is in the habit of using a magnifying glass has frequently a cramped appearance. There are also other disadvantages attendant on the habitual use of a magnifying glass. A person using such a glass must necessarily hold his head aside, so that the eye on which the glass is fixed may be directly above the part on which he is at work. In order to attain this position, the eye itself is not unfrequently distorted; and when it is kept so for any length of time it becomes extremely painful. I never find my eyes so free from pain or aching as when looking at the work directly in front, without any twisting of the neck so as to bring one eye only immediately above the part in course of execution. I therefore conclude that the eyes are less likely to be injured when thus employed than when one is frequently distorted and pained in looking through a glass. I am here merely speaking from experience, and not professedly from any theoretic knowledge of optics; but as I have hitherto done without the aid of any magnifying power, I am not without reason convinced that glasses of all kinds ought to be dispensed with until impaired vision renders their use absolutely necessary. I am decidedly of opinion that to use glasses *to preserve* the sight, is to meet half way the evil which is thus sought to be averted. A person who has his sense of hearing perfect never thinks of using a trumpet or acoustic instrument in order to preserve it. All wood engravers, whether their eyes be naturally weak or not, ought to wear a shade, similar to that represented in the following figure, No. 1, as it both protects the eyes from too strong a light, and also serves to concentrate the view on the work which the engraver is at the time engaged in executing.

When speaking on this subject, it may not be out of place to mention a kind of shade or screen for the nose and mouth, similar to that in the following figure, No. 2. Such a shade or screen is called by Papillon a *mentonnière*, and its object is to prevent the drawing on the block being injured by the breath in damp or frosty weather. Without such a precaution, a drawing made on the block with black-lead pencil would, in a great measure, be effaced by the breath of the engraver passing freely over it in such weather. Such a shade or screen is most conveniently made of a piece of thin pasteboard or stiff paper.

No. 1.

No. 2.

There are various modes of protecting the eyes when working by lamp-light, but I am aware of only one which both protects the eyes from the light and the face from the heat of the lamp. This consists in filling a large transparent glass-globe with clear water, and placing it in such a manner between the lamp and the workman that the light, after passing through the globe, may fall directly on the block, in

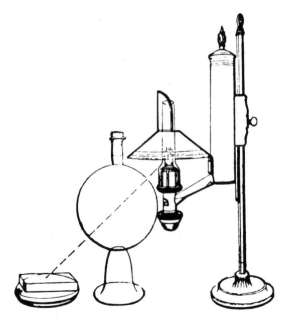

Sandbag and block. Globe.　　　　　　Lamp.

the manner represented in the preceding cut. The height of the lamp can be regulated according to the engraver's convenience, in consequence of its being moveable on the upright piece of iron or other metal which forms its support. The dotted line shows the direction of the light when the lamp is elevated to the height here seen; by lowering the lamp a little more, the dotted line would incline more to a horizontal direction, and enable the engraver to sit at a greater distance. By the use of these globes one lamp will suffice for three or four persons, and each person have a much clearer and cooler light than if he had a lamp without a globe solely to himself.

* * * * *

In proceeding to engrave figures, it is advisable to commence with such as consist of little more than outline, and have no shades expressed by cross-lines. The first step in executing such a subject is to cut a white line on each side of the pencilled lines which are to remain in relief of the height of the plane surface of the block, and to form the impression when it is printed. A cut when thus engraved, and previous to the parts which are white, when printed, being cut away, or, in technical language, *blocked out*, would present the following appearance. It is, however, necessary to observe that all

the parts which require to be blocked away have been purposely retained in this cut in order to show more clearly the manner in which it is executed; for the engraver usually cuts away as he proceeds all the black masses seen within the subject. A wide margin of solid wood round the edges of the cut is, however, generally allowed to remain until a proof be taken when the engraving is finished, as it affords a support to the paper, and prevents the exterior lines of the subject from appearing too hard. This margin, where room is allowed, is separated from the engraved parts by a moderately deep and wide furrow, and is covered with a piece of paper serving as a *frisket* in taking a proof impression by means of friction. In clearing away such of the back parts in the preceding cut as require to be removed, it is necessary to proceed with great care in order to avoid breaking down or cutting through the lines which are to be left in relief. When the cut is properly cleared out and blocked away, it is then finished, and when printed will appear thus:

Sculptures and bas-reliefs of any kind are generally best represented by simple outlines, with delicate parallel lines, running horizontally, to represent the ground. The following cut is from a design by Flaxman for the front of a gold snuff-box made by Rundell and Bridge for George IV, about 1827. The subject of this design was intended to commemorate

the General Peace concluded in 1814; to the left Agriculture is seen flourishing under the auspices of Peace; while to the right a youthful figure is seen placing a wreath above the helmet of a warrior; the trophy indicates his services, and opposite to him is seated a figure of Victory. The three other sides, and the top and bottom, were also embellished with figures and ornaments in relief designed by Flaxman. The whole of the dies were cut in steel by Henning and Son—so well known to admirers of art from their beautiful reduced copies and restorations of the sculptures of the Parthenon preserved in the British Museum—and from these dies the plates of gold composing the box were struck, so that the figures appear in slight relief. A blank space was left in the top of the box for an enamel portrait of the King, which was afterwards inserted, surrounded with diamonds, and the

margin of the lid was also ornamented in the same manner. This box is perhaps the most beautiful of the kind ever executed in any country: it may justly challenge a comparison with the drinking cups by Benvenuto Cellini, the dagger shafts designed by Durer, or the salts by Hans Holbein. The process of engraving in this style is extremely simple, as it is only necessary to leave the lines drawn in pencil untouched, and to cut away the wood on each side of them. An amateur may without much trouble teach himself to execute cuts in this manner, or to engrave fac-similes of small pen-and-ink sketches such as the annexed.

*   *   *   *   *

As the greatest advantage which wood engraging possesses over copper is the effective manner in which strongly contrasted light and shade can be represented, Rembrandt's etchings,—which, like his paintings, are distinguished by the skilful management of the chiaroscuro—form excellent studies for the engraver or designer on wood who should wish to become well acquainted with the capabilities of the art. A delicate wood-cut, executed in imitation of a smooth steel-engraving of "sober grey" tone, is sure to be tame and insipid; and whenever wood engravers attempt to give to their cuts the appearance of copper or steel-plates, and neglect the peculiar advantages of their own art, they are sure to fail, notwithstanding the pains they may bestow. Their work, instead of being commended as a successful application of the peculiar means of the art, is in effect condemned by being regarded as "a clever *imitation*, of a copper-plate."

The cut of Christ and the Woman of Samaria, copied from an etching by Rembrandt, will perhaps more forcibly illustrate what has been said with respect to wood engraving being excellently adapted to effectively express strong contrasts of light and shade. The original etching—which has been faithfully copied—is a good example of Rembrandt's consummate skill in the management of chiaro-scuro; everything that he has wished to forcibly express immediately arrests the eye, while in the whole design nothing appears abrupt. The extremes of light and shade concentre in the principal figure, that of Christ, and to this everything else in the composition is either subordinate or accessory. The middle tint under the arched passage forms a medium between between the darkness of Christ's robe and the shade under the curve of the nearest arch, and the light in the front of his figure is gradually carried off to the left through the medium

of the woman and the distant buildings, which gradually approach to the colour of the paper. Were a tint, however delicate, introduced in this subject to represent the sky, the effect would be destroyed; the parts which are now so effective would appear spotted and confused, and have a crude, unfinished appearance. By the injudicious introduction of a tinted sky many wood-cuts, which would otherwise be striking and effective, are quite spoiled.

It but too frequently happens when works are illustrated with wood-cuts, that subjects are chosen which the art cannot successfuly represent. Whether the work to be illustrated be matter of fact or fiction, the designer, unless he be acquainted both with the capabilities and defects of the art, seldom thinks of more than making a drawing according to his own fancy, and never takes into consideration the means by which is has to be executed. To this inattention may be traced many failures in works illustrated with wood-cuts, and for which the engraver is censured, although he may have, with great care and skill, accomplished all that the art could effect. An artist who is desirous that his designs, when engraved on wood, should appear like impressions from *over-done* steel-plates, ought never to be employed to make drawings for wood engravers: he does not understand the peculiar advantages of the art, and his designs will only have a tendency to bring it into contempt, while those who execute them will be blamed for the defects which are the result of his want of knowledge.

Thomas Gilks

The Art of Wood-Engraving: a Practical Handbook
1866. pp. 36-53

How to Blend Tints.

Tints are many and various, according to the subject and taste of the worker. Our illustration [on p. 138] is a slight combination of the straight tint or blue sky with a few clouds, the difference arising chiefly from the tools used. The dry, hard, wavy and mechanical line seen in old cuts of thirty years ago, is now superseded by clouds formed of short lines blended by the pressure of the graver rather than the tint tool. Although different tint tools are generally used, yet a skilful engraver will produce by various degrees of

THE ART

OF

WOOD ENGRAVING.

A PRACTICAL HAND-BOOK.

BY

THOMAS GILKS.

WITH NUMEROUS ILLUSTRATIONS BY THE AUTHOR.

SIXTH EDITION.

Ars probat artificem.

LONDON:

WINSOR & NEWTON, Limited, 38, RATHBONE PLACE.

pressure very different lines with one tool—in fact the roundness or fulness of clouds can only be naturally produced by
graver-work in short pieces delicately blended together by
very fine gravers.

One of the most remarkable differences between old-
fashioned and modern landscape wood engraving is the
refinement to which the Art is now brought—the old-fashioned
engine-turned kind of wave tint being quite superseded by
the modern mode of blending short lines, with stops between
them. Some of the most exquisite effects are frequently the
result of carefully making use of the wood originally left
(technically called "*stops*,") in the first working of the sky
tints. Of course, this presupposes taste and artistic feeling on
the part of the engraver, as well as careful manipulative skill;
and in working this out, above everything it is necessary that
the *fine graver* used in working upon these junctions should
be kept quite sharp. If this is attended to, a richness of tone
in the various kinds of tint will be the result, and only the
most practised eye would detect the means that have been so
satisfactorily employed to produce it.

How to Shade and Show Roundness.

The illustration of a globe, or ball, will best explain a very simple mode of lining to be adopted in showing roundness. This is done by gravers of different degrees of width, bearing in mind our former remarks, that in proportion to the pressure of the hand will be the depth or width of the line, so that in the dark shade, or that immediately proceeding from the black, the pressure upon the tool must be very slight.

In working out this lesson of roundness by graver shading, let the student place before him examples like a bright polished round tea-pot, or kettle, or a vase, or egg—or, in fact, any object of similar character and shape. Place the same in strong sun or lamp light, and then carefully watch how, immediately behind the highest light, the deepest shadow (or touch of solid black) gradually resolves into grey

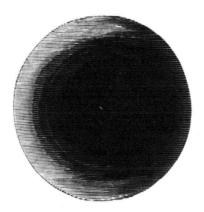

and then recedes at the edge into a *reflected* light. Let the student carefully imitate these several objects with the graver in the way we have indicated, and by that time he will have mastered the lesson of "How to shade, so as to produce roundness."

This kind of shading had better be carefully understood from the first, as, in the carrying out of nearly every kind of figure work, roundness will more or less have to be shown.

How to Shade and Show Concavity.

An ordinary basin which we have made use of in our illustration will explain the mode of lining requisite in concavity, or to show anything hollow. To represent this correctly, a line is necessary, the reverse of that which illustrates solid roundness.

In the rather rude illustration of our meaning, shown in the above cut, it will be at once seen that the light strikes the top of the basin in the inside, and gradually merges into total darkness without any reflected light, as in the case of rotundity or the round ball. We have lined this vessel from the top, curving the line with the shape of the inside of the basin, but so that the graduated shadow is preserved with the cavity of the object—any mode of placing the graver line will effect the same end. Let the student, however, carefully practise upon several differently shaped hollow subjects, such as an *open* tea-pot, tea-cup, a jar, or the centre of any like object; let him work it out by regular lines, and he will soon, as in the former case, be enabled to express what he wishes to convey by graver lines.

This lesson it is equally important fully to understand as the former; as all lines should assist faithfully to express the form intended; and the working it out properly will well

repay trouble, for in most subjects concavity will hav\
shown as frequently as roundness.

How to Engrave a Shaded Figure Subject.

In the annexed illustration [over] we have filled up with work
that same subject used by us to explain outline engraving:
merely shading it with a simple kind of line, and fac-simile best
fitted to show the forms of the figure, and other parts, and
not difficult for a learner to work out for himself. In a subject
like this, every line and touch will be placed for the engraver
in the drawing upon the wood. He will commence the engraving at the upper part and work downwards, and in his progress
will always bear in mind which is the light side, and which
the shadow side of the figure. In the light side, thin and refine
up all the lines, while on the shadow side of the work the
wood must not be over-refined, or cut away. In engraving
faces and hands, knowledge of drawing is most essential;
great care must be taken not to cut away the wood showing
the features, as expression is given or taken away in proportion to the poverty or richness of the line left. As a rule,
leave plenty of colour in the under parts of the nose and
mouth, and in the shadows cast by the fingers in their opening, of separating one from the other, also at the knuckles,
&c. In the subject annexed, it will be observed that on the
shadow side of the figure, or dog, or pitcher, portions of
solid black are left—this colour tends to give roundness,
while the slight reflected lights on the same side help also in
rounding the object. In the pencilling to denote foliage, be
careful to reproduce the thick and thin character of the line
made, as in such like sketchy drawings much depends on the
line being engraved thick and thin, exactly as drawn; too
much stress cannot be laid on this observation, as a drawing
seemingly sketchy and careless is frequently the result of
much forethought, very suggestive, and fitted for the purposes
intended.

In the manipulation of the figures contained in the above lesson, we have, perhaps, elaborated the kind of work more than was strictly necessary in order to make our meaning clear, and that the student should see at a glance wherein consists richness in the mode of pencilling; also, to show texture of material and other characteristic appearances. The kind of cross-hatching to be found in the dress of the elder girl is calculated, if properly done, to give force and richness to the drawing of the figure—this work must not, however, run too closely into the deep shadows, which should be picked out crisp, square, and solid black; and then the black lends force to the fac-simile work, and *vice versa*.

It will be seen that some of the cross-lines to which we have referred have a dot, or line in the centre. This dot, or line, is intended to give a tone, or undertint, to the work, and in outlining the cross lines with a graver, great care should be observed not to injure the form of these dots or lines, or the tone will be destroyed; additional richness is given to any piece of drapery or dress made up of this kind of work.

How to Engrave a Landscape.

The accompanying cut of Llanberris Pass will show a cloudy sky, and the direction of lines to be observed in engraving rocks as well as mountains. In a subject like this, certain artistic taste and skill on the part of the engraver are essential, as in the drawing upon wood the light and shade of the subject will be partly washed in, while the rough foreground rocks and grass *only* will be pencilled in fac-simile manner. Most of the remaining parts will be merely indicated by direction pencil lines upon the washes; thus, in the *graver* work, great care must be taken to show by the direction of the line, whether it is the upper part of the mountain, a grass slope, or the chipped and broken side of the mountain, that is to be represented, as each and all of the separate parts will require their special mode of treatment. As landscapes

Pass of Llanberris.

are so various in character, we can only again urge the learner
to attend to the observations we have before made upon the
different sorts of work to be executed, whether *roundness*
or *concavity* be intended, whether distance or foreground,
not forgetting the texture of the work; each and all the parts
must show thought, and then the simplest form of manipulation with the graver, expressing what is intended, will be
better and more successful than the most elaborate work
done in a mere mechanical manner, without reflecting upon
what purpose or purposes it is to serve or express.

In the refinement or finishing up of a landscape like the
accompanying illustration, or even one of a more elaborate
character, the student must always bear in mind that working
upon it without meaning is neither finish nor refinement of
work, but frequently the reverse. It is much better to leave
"well" alone, even in the *rough*, than to fritter away the
effect by "touching up" and seeming refinement without any
definite result. Turner, the great landscape painter, when he
was once asked to define "finish," is reported to have
answered, "when he considered himself to be making progress;" and further to have said, when he failed in that, he

"*stopped work*." In finishing or refining landscapes, or, in fact, any other kind of engraving on wood, we would strongly impress Turner's most useful rule on the student's mind: better *stop*, if you cannot see your way to more real finish, than go on in the dark.

In much of the *modern* and *fashionable* wood engraving (if we may use such a term) we are ready to admit there is much elaboration; but we feel bound at the same time to say, much of that *elaboration* is at the expense of *artistic feeling*, which might frequently express itself more fervently by simpler means.

This lesson is illustrated by a second plate, a view of Airey Force, which shows the method of engraving rocks so distinctly, that no particular instructions are necessary.

Fac-simile and Portrait Engraving.

If the learner has carefully worked out the foregoing examples, he will be to a certain extent prepared for our final illustration, or, that which we have placed at the frontispiece of this Handbook. It is intended to explain "cross-hatching," and fac-simile work on a portrait. This technical term, "cross-hatching," means pencil lines crossing each other in various ways, the production of which in copper-engraving is simple and easy enough, but it requires much experience and patience to execute them with precision and delicacy on wood. In the first place, the drawing has to be very carefully made upon the wood, and it is the engraver's province to reproduce every dot and cross line the artist has drawn, which he can only do by cutting away all the lozenge-shaped interstices. To effect this, a lozenge-shaped graver is used, and the white square of wood between the pencil lines is cleanly removed with two cuts of the tool inserted at opposite angles. This rule, however, only applies to "cross-hatching" in its simplest form, for much of modern wood engraving is made up of more elaborate manipulation than that above described; for instance, when several lines intersect each other, then very

Airey Force, Ulleswater.

great care is required, so that the lines *when engraved* shall show those intersections in the same way as the drawing.

We do not wish in any way to recommend *unmeaning* "cross-hatching" either on a *face*, or on any parts of the dress, or drapery generally—the chief object of this lesson is, that wherever this kind of work is to be done, our assistance shall enable the student to work it out with understanding and skill.

Faces, of all parts of the human figure, it is most important to understand fully, and to engrave with feeling and taste. When the drawing is correct and carefully lined over with the pencil, follow out all the lines with great care, as has been done in the frontispiece illustration, to which we again direct the learner's careful attention. In all portrait engravings, great care should be especially taken to leave plenty of colour in all the principal parts of the face that are intended to mark expression—such as the pupils of the eyes, the nostril, and under-part of the nose, the under-part of the lip, &c. If the wood is not too much refined away—whatever might be said to the contrary by *weak* criticism, the Art of wood engraving is capable of producing a more artistic portrait—a portrait more satisfying to the lover of true art than any of the more polished and smoother processes.

It becomes necessary here to describe an operation employed for the production of roundness and delicacy. It is called white cross-lining, in contra-distinction to black cross-lining. Thus, when the ordinary lines have been cut, a finer graver, or more frequently a very fine tint tool, is used to cross the work already engraved. Then with the fine tool cross the lines first at an angle with the ordinary work, and afterwards recross them so as to produce a lozenge (never a square) in thin white lines. This, if carried out with judgment, keeping in view always a definite result—will produce not only increased roundness in the subjects so worked upon, such as hands, feet, faces, and flesh generally, but will give a great degree of minute finish; yet this finish must be fully felt or not attempted. We have seen much good work spoiled by young engravers attempting what they were unable to accomplish—as a rule, therefore, the use of the white cross-lines should be exceptional.

We are quite aware it is considered that portrait work is not the true province of wood engraving, and perhaps the objectors are right, if the art attempts the polished processes of a smooth copper-plate; but, in its own way, and by its own legitimate method, nothing is finer, or more truly artistic, than a well drawn and simply engraved wood-cut portrait.

W. J. Linton

Wood-Engraving. A Manual of Instruction
1884. pp. 81-85

Of Beauty of Line.

Out of an impressionist school of painting, and subservient to the conditions of the impressionists, has arisen a school of impressionist engraving, the perfection of the imbecile. I find no other word so fit to characterize the process. The piece of work below is an exact reproduction (not enlarged) of part of a "cloudy sky" in a recent number of an art-paper. It may serve as text for our chapter upon BEAUTY OF LINE. I doubt not that the draughtsman with certain hasty washes of the brush drew in this sky in such carelessly impressive manner as is here apparent in the work of the engraver, whose lines perhaps have not unfaithfully followed even the directions suggested by the brush. Does anyone

"Cloud".

think that the lines here given, however suggested or set in order by the artistic brush, are in any sense fit to represent a cloudy sky? Do they at all present it to us? In good engraving there must be always fitness of line. Good engraving is the forming of a picture by fit lines. And fitness of line will always lead to beauty. I can not think of a good engraving but as a work of beauty, a work of high art, however it may be disparaged by those without artistic knowledge to lift them to its comprehension.

The bit of "engraving" I give here is perhaps an extreme, but it is not an unfair instance of the kind of work which I have said has come into vogue through what is called the "Impressionist School" of painting. Some young men, lacking neither cleverness nor conceit, persuaded themselves that much labour, close study, and thoroughness, were not requisite. They made admirable sketches in colour, and thought them as good as finished pictures. The sketches were finished enough to give you a pleasant impression of the painter's intention; and what could be more desired? The world cares for sketches by the elder Titian; why should not the sketches of the younger Titian, just fresh from school, be cared for equally? Conceit is daring, and daring commands, when it may not deserve success. The young Titians forthwith set the fashion: they praised each other, crowed much, and friendly young art critics joined in the jubilation. Let it be said that these impressionist painters, whose headquarters were of late in New York, may perhaps have deserved praise for their departure from the hackneyed ways of their elders; let it be admitted that their most unfinished paintings have all the merit claimed for them. That does not concern me here. But it does concern me, and concerns my teaching, that these same painters began to draw for engravers, and to draw upon wood, and with this sketchy work of theirs inaugurated "a new era in engraving," the results of which may be best studied in the two American magazines, *Harper's Monthly* and the *Century*.

Our older draughtsmen on wood, the poorest as the most talented, with very few exceptions, had all one virtue—their drawings were careful. They were not sketches, but drawings. A drawing on the block by W. L. Leitch (the landscape painter), or by Duncan, was as beautifully complete, as carefully finished as a water-colour painting. The drawings of Thurston and of Harvey were of the same perfection. George Cruikshank's drawings were as clear as his etchings, perhaps more precise. But the new men have been, and are, disdainful of this drudgery. Yet, with a strange inconsistency, while insisting that any hasty and unconsidered sketch is good enough to be engraved from, they require from the engraver a slavish adherence to the slightest and most trifling accidents, and most flagrant errors of their crude performances. From this unsatisfactory pretence of drawing, coupled with the unfortunate use of photography, instead of drawing on wood, has proceeded the present degradation of the art. Will the art-critic open his eyes? Everywhere one hears it said, authoritatively, and repeatedly, as if there could be no doubt: "What a wonderful advance has been lately made in wood-engraving!" I protest, unhesitatingly and positively. If I know what engraving is, or should be, this vaunted "advance" must be condemned as retrograde, and as the degradation of the Art.

Here, by way of parenthesis, let me acknowledge the ability of both artists and engravers whose work I have to criticize. There are perhaps at this time in America as many artists who could draw on wood, and as many engravers capable of good work, as have been known in the art for the last fifty years. It is not the men I would attack, but the method of work they have adopted or submitted to. And when I refer to America especially, it is not that I recognize the "new" method as of American invention, but because in America has sprung up the claim to regard it as most excellent, and in the pages of the two magazines I have named, I find its most notable examples.

I have cared throughout all my teaching, and endeavoured in my practice, to insist upon the recognition of engraving as an art. I find nothing I can honestly call art in the "new departure" or "new development," by whichever name it may be known. I find a most marvellously successful mechanism, which is not an advance in *art*. Let my reader take any number of the *Century* or *Harper*, and try if he can discover (except in the portraits, and some few other cuts, I cannot remember many) *any lines that have beauty, or fitness, or any sign of intelligence.* Colour is kept admirably; delicacy—that is, fineness, thinness of line—is most remarkable; the often needless, sometimes unhappy, minuteness is astonishing. I am surprised at these accomplishments, often exceeding what I thought possible in wood-engraving. It is the triumphant assertion of mechanical skill. What eyes these men must have! what nicety of hand! But then . . .

I have to speak as an engraver. In the prettiest and most successful of these engravings I look in vain for anything to tell me that the engraver had any brains; that he could have known or understood the forms he was engraving; that he had any thought of perspective, any perception of differences of substance. In nearly all the cuts the foreground objects are on the same plane as those in the background—there is neither air nor distance; sky may be wall, and water may be folds of drapery, for any difference of treatment; and the lines throughout are laid with utter disregard of the things to be represented by them, in seeming ignorance or wilful rejection of all the laws of linear beauty and perspective recognized and cared for by the masters of engraving, both in wood and copper. The horizontal lines of a sky are crossed perpendicularly; the bark of a tree, a woman's cheek or bosom, a sheep's back, have no distinction of line to denote difference of substance; foreground and distance are cut with the same unvarying fineness; all things stick together; all things are undefined, muddled, confused. Colour, I have said, is excellently kept; and your first impression, not noticing the lines, taking the picture only as a clever and very exact imitation of a photograph, may strike you very pleasantly; but if you return to it, if you examine it, you will get no satisfaction from it. The enduring pleasure of a beautiful engraving it will not give you. Forget the lines altogether, it may be possible to like it; but you will not care to look at it again and again. The more closely you examine it, the greater will be your disappointment. Does not that of itself condemn it?

Mason Jackson

The Pictorial Press

1885. pp. 315-324

In describing the production of a modern pictorial newspaper, I take the *Illustrated London News* as the type of its class, because it was the first paper of the kind that was ever established. The art of wood-engraving, to which the illustrated newspaper owes its existence, has been fully described by competent authors. The best work on the subject is that

THE
PICTORIAL PRESS
ITS ORIGIN AND PROGRESS.

BY

MASON JACKSON.

With One Hundred and Fifty Illustrations.

LONDON:

HURST AND BLACKETT, PUBLISHERS,

13 GREAT MARLBOROUGH STREET.

1885.

produced by the late John Jackson in 1839; but since that date the resources of the art have been greatly developed, chiefly through the influence of illustrated newspapers.

The material used for wood-engraving is box-wood, which is preferred to all other kinds of wood on account of its close grain, hardness, and light colour. It admits of finer and sharper lines being cut upon it than any other wood, and great quantities are consumed in producing the engravings of an illustrated newspaper. According to Mr. J. R. Jackson, Curator of the Kew Museum, the box-tree is at the present time widely distributed through Europe and Asia, being found abundantly in Italy, Spain, Southern France, and on the coast of the Black Sea, as well as China, Japan, Northern India, and Persia. The box of English growth is so small as to be almost useless for commercial purposes. What is called Turkey box-wood is the best, and this is all obtained from the forests that grow on the Caucasus, and is chiefly shipped at Poti and Rostoff. The forests extend from thirty to a hundred and eighty miles inland, but many of them are in the hands of the Russian Government and are closed to commerce. Within the last few years a supply of box-wood has been obtained from the forests in the neighbourhood of the Caspian Sea; but Turkey box is becoming dearer every year and inferior in quality. After the wood is cut in the forest, it is brought down on horseback to the nearest river, put on board flat-bottom boats, and floated down to the port of shipment. It arrives in this country either at Liverpool or London, chiefly the former, and is usually in logs about four feet long and eight or ten inches across.

The wood intended for engraving purposes is first carefully selected and then cut up into transverse slices about an inch thick. After being cut, the pieces are placed in racks something like plate-racks, and thoroughly seasoned by slow degrees in gradually heated rooms. This seasoning process ought to last, on an average, four or five years; but the exigencies of trade seldom allow of so long a time. They are then cut into parallelograms of various sizes, the outer portion of the circular section near the bark being cut away, and all defective wood rejected. These parallelograms are then assorted as to size, and fitted together at the back by brass bolts and nuts. By this means blocks of any size can be made, and they possess the great advantage of being capable of being taken to pieces after a drawing is made, and distributed among as many engravers as there are pieces in the block. This invention of making bolted blocks was brought forward just about the time the *Illustrated London News* was started, when large blocks and quick engraving came to be in demand. In the days of the *Penny Magazine*, blocks were made by simply glueing the pieces of wood together, or they were fastened by means of a long bolt passing through the entire block.

The cut given below represents the back of a half-page block of the *Illustrated London News*, and shows the way in which the bolts and nuts are used for fastening the different parts of the block together.

For the production of a pictorial newspaper a large staff of

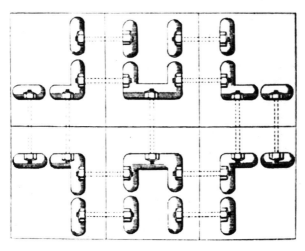

Back of a block, showing the way in which the parts
are fastened together.

draughtsmen and engravers is required, who must be ready at a moment's notice to take up any subject, and, if necessary, work day and night until it is done. The artist who supplies the sketch has acquired by long practice a rapid method of working, and can, by a few strokes of his pencil, indicate a passing scene by a kind of pictorial short-hand, which is afterwards translated and extended in the finished drawing. The sketch being completed on paper, the services of the draughtsman on wood come into requisition, for it is not often that the drawing on the block is made by the same person who supplies the sketch. Sometimes the sketch to be dealt with is the production of an amateur, or is so hastily or indifferently done that it has to be remodelled or rearranged in drawing it on the wood. Faulty or objectionable portions have to be left out or subdued, and perhaps a point in the sketch that is quite subordinate, is brought forward and made to form a prominent part of the picture. All this has to be done without doing violence to the general truth of the representation, and with due consideration for the particular conditions of the moment, such as the amount of finish and distribution of light and shade suitable for rapid engraving and printing.

An example of the adaptation of a rapid sketch occurs in the engraving of the surrender of Sedan, published in the *Illustrated London News*, September 17, 1870. This sketch, which carries with it the strongest evidence of being taken 'under fire,' came to hand a few hours before the engravings for the current week were to be ready for the printer. The cream or heart of the sketch, representing an officer waving a white flag over the gate of Sedan attended by a trumpeter, was taken for the subject, while the comparatively unimportant part of the sketch was left out. The drawing was rapidly executed and as rapidly engraved, and was ready for press at the usual time. I give [over] a reduced copy of the engraving, together with a facsimile reduction of the original sketch, which will show the reader the way in which hurried sketches are sometimes adapted to the purposes of a newspaper without at all impairing their original truth.

Sometimes more than one draughtsman is employed on a drawing where the subject consists of figures and landscape, or figures and architecture. In such a case, if time presses, the two parts of the drawing are proceeded with simultaneously. The whole design is first traced on the block; the bolts at the back of the block are then loosened, the parts are separated, and the figure-draughtsman sets to work on his division of the block, while another draughtsman is busied with the landscape or architecture, as the case may be. Occasionally, when there is very great hurry, the block is separated piece by piece as fast as the parts of the drawing are finished—the engraver and draughtsman thus working on the same subject at the same time. Instances have occurred where the draughtsman has done his work in this way, and has never seen the whole of his drawing together. The double-page engraving of the marriage of the Prince of Wales in the *Illustrated London News*, March 21, 1863, was drawn on the wood by Sir John Gilbert at 198 Strand, and as fast as each part of the drawing was done it was separated from the rest and given to the engraver. Considering that the artist never saw his drawing entire, it is wonderful to find the engraving so harmonious and effective. Photographing on the wood is now in general use for portraits, sculpture, architecture, and other subjects where there is a picture or finished drawing on paper to work from.

The drawing on wood being completed, it passes into the hands of the engraver, and the first thing he does is to cut or *set* the lines across all the joins of the block before the different parts are distributed among the various engravers. This is done partly to ensure as far as possible some degree of harmony of colour and texture throughout the subject. When all the parts are separated and placed in the hands of different engravers each man has thus a sort of *key-note* to guide him in the execution of his portion, and it should be

The surrender of Sedan. From the 'Illustrated London news,'
Sept. 17, 1870.

his business to imitate and follow with care the colour and
texture of the small pieces of engraving which he finds already
done at the edge of his part of the block where it joins the
rest of the design. The accompanying cuts represent a block
entire and the same subject divided.

Though this system of subdividing the engraving effects a
great saving of time, it must be admitted that it does not
always result in the production of a first-rate work of art as
a whole. For, supposing the subject to be a landscape with a

Facsimile of sketch: surrender of Sedan.

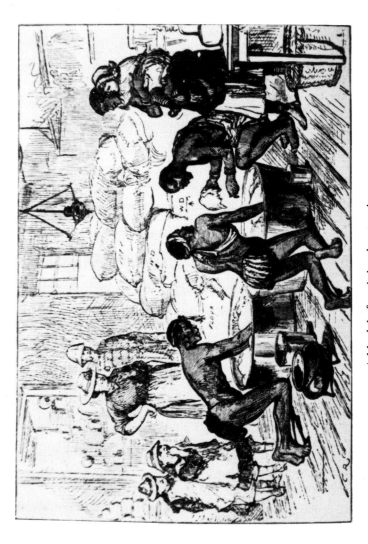

A block before it is taken to pieces.

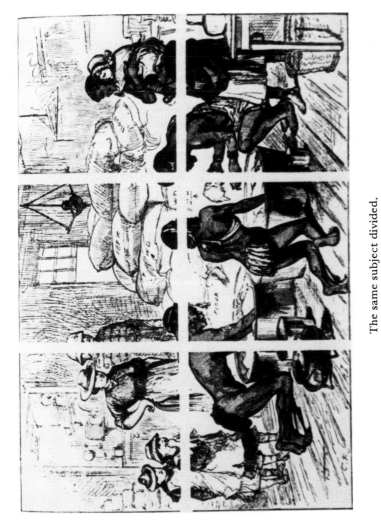

The same subject divided.

good stretch of trees, the two or three engravers who have the trees to engrave have, perhaps, each a different method of rendering foliage; and when the whole is completed, and the different pieces are put together, the trees perhaps appear like a piece of patchwork, with a distinct edge to each man's work. To harmonise and dovetail (so to speak) these different pieces of work is the task of the superintending artist, who retouches the first proof of the engraving and endeavours to blend together the differences of colour and texture. This is often no easy task, for the press is generally waiting, and the time that is left for such work is often reduced to minutes where hours would scarcely suffice to accomplish all that might be done. Or the block to be engraved may be a marine subject, with a stormy sea. In this case, like the landscape, two or three engravers may be employed upon the water, each of them having a different way of representing that element. Here it is even more difficult than in the landscape to blend the conflicting pieces of work, and requires an amount of 'knocking about' that sometimes astonishes the original artist. All this is the necessary result of the hurry in which the greater part of newspaper engravings have to be produced. When the conditions are more favourable better things are successfully attempted, and of this the illustrated newspapers of the day have given abundant proofs.

It is obvious that when a block is divided and the parts are distributed in various hands, if any accident should occur to one part the whole block is jeopardised. It is much to the credit of the fraternity of engravers that this rarely or ever happens. I only remember one instance of a failure of this kind within my own experience. An engraver of decidedly Bohemian character, after a hard night's work on the tenth part of a page block, thought fit to recruit himself with a cheering cup. In the exhilaration that followed he lost the piece of work upon which he had been engaged, and thereby rendered useless the efforts of himself and his nine compatriots.

William Smith

Advertise. How? When? Where?

1863. pp. 16-19, 86-89

Railways, &c.

Every one must be familiar with the sketch in *Punch* of the two colliers at the Wednesbury Station:—

"*First Collier.*—Trains leave for Birmingham, 10.23 A.M., 6.30 P.M.

"*Second Collier.*—What's P.M.?

"*First do.*—A penny a mile to be sure.

"*Second do.*—Then what's A.M.?

"*First do.*—Why that must be a 'apenny a mile."

How many of us have been equally puzzled in finding out the arrival and departure of trains to a small station of a branch line. Where is the man that is bold enough to say that he is thoroughly conversant with Bradshaw? If there is one, let him now stand forth. I remember an anecdote of a country farmer coming to see his London cousin, who kept a grocer's shop in Barbican. He arrived on the Saturday morning; the shop was full of customers, and his cousin took him to an inner room, and told the shop-boy to take in some ale and a newspaper. The boy got the former, but not succeeding in the latter, gave the country friend "Bradshaw" to read. His cousin, when the customers slackened, went to join him, and said:—"Oh, that's all right, you've been reading. What is it?—how do you like it?" "Oh," he replied, "it's a very interesting book, but rather too many figures. I can't make it out!"—Who can? The present time-tables are a sealed book. The main lines, with the intermediate stations, should be in one column, and the branches in another. In every railway carriage, there should be a map of the rail, with the

distance from station to station, and a shifting scroll to say—
This train stops at *Norwood, Croydon,* &c.
Change for *Grinstead, Horsham.*

And at every station should be painted, in bold figures, the distance from London, and to the next place, and so on. The railway company could save their expense of getting up

and printing the new time-tables by having a neat border round, with a space for advertisements. All the great firms would be glad of such a medium. By night, the stations might have a neat transparency to state the time of departure and destination of trains. It would be a trifling expense to the company, but a great accommodation to the public. When space would allow, it would be a boon to have an extra·office to take tickets for excursions three or four days before; or, a place might be opened opposite the station, similar to the ticket-offices of Her Majesty's and Covent Garden Theatres. Numbers would be induced to take tickets who, when they had purchased, would not allow them to be lost, and would be sure and get up in time on the Sunday morning.

If the railway companies felt inclined they could improve

the unsightly appearance of the iron bridges that are crossing all our streets, by renting them to the respectable firms for advertising, compelling the renters to have well painted boards of one uniform size with handsome moulding; the spaces would be very readily taken. If at every station there were a glass transparency, with shifting signals, it might occasionally prevent accidents, &c. &c. They could be made with very little expense—

Express Train Started 5 minutes	Luggage Train at next Station

the letters cut out of zinc to work in a groove in the glass box.

* * * * *

That summer is more advantageous than winter, as a general rule, every one must be aware; and in considering "when to advertise," due regard should be paid to the time of year, the weather, as also to the number of excursions, fêtes, reviews, and alfresco entertainments generally. Yet at times, during the short days, there is a large amount of business done in the delivery of bills, books, &c., &c. I will give one instance which occurred during the Cattle Show week of 1861:—

I started on the Thursday morning from the Elephant and Castle to the Railway-station, London-bridge; over the bridge, down Cannon-street, to the office of the *Times*; through the Temple-gardens, along the left-hand side of the Strand, to the Adelphi Theatre. From there to the bottom of Parliament-street, through the Park and Sloane-street, returning down Piccadilly, Coventry-street, across Leicester-square, Long-acre, Great Queen-street, Holborn-hill, along Smithfield, to the (then) Eastern Counties Railway; back down Bishopsgate-street, Cornhill, Cheapside, Ludgate-hill, Fleet-street, along

WALL-POSTING AS IT IS.

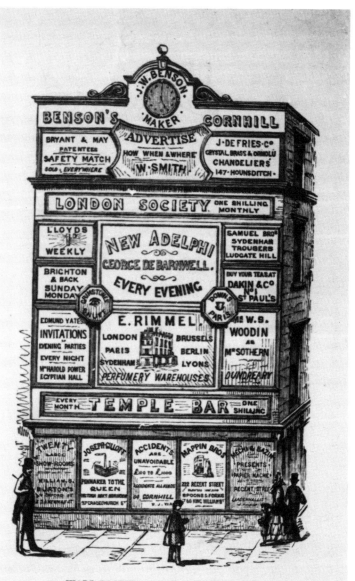

WALL-POSTING AS IT OUGHT TO BE.

the right-hand side of the Strand, Waterloo-place, Regent-street, Oxford-street, Baker-street, to the Bazaar; and then returned to the Adelphi Theatre by the same route, but on the opposite side of the road.

During my journey I took every bill, book, or pamphlet that was offered me, and on my arriving at my destination I had in all two hundred and fifty. The average number of pedestrians that would pass the bill-deliverers in the route given, from 10 a.m. to 7 p.m., would amount to 40,000—(that is certainly under the mark). If only one-half of the passersby took half of the bills, &c., given away, the number distributed would amount, in the nine hours, to two millions three hundred thousand!

If we make the calculation on the same scale for the year, allowing for Sundays, wet and foggy days, and reckoning, say eight months, or 250 days, out of the 365, they would amount to the almost incredible number of 575,000,000! Then we have to take into consideration besides, that I did not in my walks pass more than the half of the London bill-deliverers, and only touched at one of the railway stations— (at the South Western Station, Waterloo-road, 1500 bills are given away daily during the summer); so, if we double the number, 1,150,000,000 are distributed.

On Wednesday, December 10, 1862, I went to the Smithfield Cattle Show, at the Agricultural Hall, Islington; and during the two hours I was in the building I received—

69 bills,
27 books,
8 cards,

Making $\overline{104}$

The number of illustrations in the same amounted to 475.

Now 50,000 persons visited the building on that day, so if we calculate as before, that half the number took half the bills, &c., it would make 1,300,000 bills, books, and cards distributed in one day's show!

In fact, when we go on thus piling up figures, getting into

such denominations as *thousands of millions* (!) we feel lost among the enormous statistics, and begin to think that the total number of bills, cards, books, &c., given away from one year's end to another is, as my Lord Dundreary would say, "one of those things *no* fellah can make out."

You will occasionally on a wet or snowy day, when you would not even turn out a stray cat, see a poor and not too warmly-clad old man, standing at the corner of a street,

mechanically offering a bill, when not a single person is seen, except the wet policeman, plodding along his damp and dreary beat.

That is decidedly *not* the time or place to advertise; nor is a tombstone in a churchyard the exact spot to expect a six-sheet poster or a double-crown bill. Yet in the North of England, in a burial-ground belonging to one of our old ivy-porched churches, was, and perhaps is, an elegantly-carved tombstone, on which is inscribed an excellent advertisement—not of the virtues of the departed, but of the business of the living—

"Sacred to the memory of John Roberts, Stonemason and tombcutter, who died on Saturday, October the 8th, 1800. N.B.—The business carried on by the widow, at No. 1, Fresh-field-place."

Philip Gilbert Hamerton

The Graphic Arts

1882. pp. xiii-xvi, 1-3

Lithography is slightly esteemed because it has been vulgarised by feeble work, or by work that is manually skilful, but destitute of mental originality. It is also very unfortunate in being frequently represented by impressions from worn stones. It has become a business, and a business not always conducted with a due regard even to a commercial reputation. But surely this unlucky turn in the application of the art has nothing to do with its higher capabilities? It was heartily appreciated by great men in the last generation. If such men as Decamps, Géricault, and Delacroix, practised it or approved of it, we may be quite sure that it is an artist's process, whether it may happen to be fashionable in the present day, or applied to unfashionable uses.

I am told now that woodcut, though popular enough in a practical way as an adjunct to journalism, and a handmaid of scientific literature, is despised by the aesthetic taste of the day. Like lithography, it has become a trade; careful drawings are often cut to pieces by apprentices, and badly printed

afterwards. We may deplore these errors. It is always sad to
see good materials turned to unworthy uses, but these mis-
applications ought not to make us unjust to the art which is
pursued unworthily. Is literature always followed with a due
sense of its noblest responsibilities and powers? Woodcut can
be printed cheaply, so that it is used and abused in commerce,
yet it has fine artistic capabilities. It is not a painter's process,
because it is too laborious for an occupied painter to undertake it; but it is a thoroughly sound process, capable of the
most various effects; and it has been encouraged by great
artists, especially by Holbein, too delicate a draughtsman to
patronise a rude and imperfect art.

The fundamental error in estimating the Graphic Arts is
to rank them by comparison with the ineffable completeness
of nature. They may be compared with nature; they shall be
so compared in this volume, but only as a matter of scientific
curiosity, not at all for the purpose of condemning some arts
and exalting others. We who are constantly accustomed to
the language—or, rather, in the plural, the very different
languages—of the graphic arts, lose by familiarity with their
meaning the sense of their real remoteness from nature. We
forget—we become incapable of properly understanding—
what a distance there is between the natural object and the
artistic representation. For example, it was the custom of
the old masters in many of their drawings to shade in strong,
open, diagonal lines. There is nothing in nature like that.
It is simply a conventional language intended to convey the
notion of shade without imitation, without even the beginning of an imitation, of its qualities. This is a single instance,
but I could fill a hundred pages with such instances. If imitative truth were the test of excellence in the fine arts, the
greater part of the drawings, etchings, and engravings in our
museums, and many of the pictures in our galleries, would
have to be condemned without remission. The real test of
excellence in a process is this. Will it conveniently—that is,
without too much troublesome technical embarrassment—

express human knowledge and human feeling? Will it record in an intelligible manner the results of human observation? If it will do this for man, with reference to some limited department of nature only, such as form, or light and dark, or colour without full natural light, then it is a good art, however far it may fall short of nature in a vain struggle for complete imitation. This is the reason why we value so many drawings by great artists in which they voluntarily bridled the imitative instinct. They restrained that instinct; they pulled it up at some point fixed in each case by some special artistic purpose and by the nature of the materials that they employed. *They* did not share the scorn for limited means of expression, which is one of the signs of imperfect culture, but they looked upon each tool as a special instrument and employed it in accordance with its proper uses, content if it expressed their thought, often not less content if the thought were conveyed by a hint or a suggestion to intelligences not very far inferior to their own.

In our own time an entirely new set of processes have rendered service by reproducing drawings and engravings of various kinds, often with a remarkable degree of fidelity. Some of these processes have been employed in the illustration of the present volume, and great care has been taken, by the rejection of failures, to have the best results which the present condition of photographic engraving could afford. The reader may be glad to know how these reproductions have been made. Without entering into details which would require many pages for their explanation, I may say that the processes used for this volume are of very different natures. That employed by Messrs. Goupil, called *photogravure*, is a secret, and all I know about it is that the marvellously intelligent inventor discovered some means of making a photograph in which all the darks stood in proportionate relief, and from which a cast in electrotype could be taken which would afterwards serve as a plate to print from. All the Goupil photogravures in this volume are so produced, and very wonderful things they are, especially the Mercury, which is the most difficult feat of reproduction I have hitherto seen attempted, on account of the extreme delicacy of many lines and the sharpness of others. We also give plates printed in two or more colours. They are printed in each case from one copper and with one turn of the press; *how*, we are unable to explain, but though the making of these illustrations is mysterious, the quality of them will be admitted by everyone who knows the originals in the Louvre. M. Dujardin's process of *héliogravure* is entirely different. He covers a plate made of a peculiar kind of bronze with a sensitive ground, and after photographing the subject on that simply etches it and has it retouched with the burin if required. M. Amand Durand employs ordinary copper plates, and uses bichromatised gelatine as an etching ground, which acquires various degrees of insolubility by exposure to light. He bites his plates like ordinary etchings; and when they are intended to represent etchings he rebites them in the usual way and works upon them with dry point, &c., just as an etcher does, but when they represent engravings he finishes them with the burin. In the reproductions from Mr. Poynter's drawings, in this volume, the dark lines are done by photographic etching, and the uniform ground, which imitates Mr. Poynter's paper, is in ordinary aquatint. The reader now perceives the essential difference between the Goupil Process, in which there is no etching, and the processes employed by the *héliograveurs*, which are entirely founded upon etching.

The mechanical autotype process is founded upon the absorption of moisture by partially soluble gelatine, and its rejection by bichromatised gelatine rendered insoluble by exposure to light. The printing is done in oil ink, which is rejected by the moist gelatine and caught by the insoluble. In the reproduction of a pen drawing the ink lines are printed from portions of gelatine which have been rendered insoluble by the action of light, and the blank spaces between the lines represent the moistened gelatine. This is an excellent process for many purposes, certainly the best of all for the imitation of pen drawings.

The most defective of all photographic processes are generally those intended to print like woodcuts in the text. Such reproductions often abound in thickened or in broken lines, or in lines run together, and when this is the case they are worse than worthless from a critical point of view. The few reproductions printed with the text in the present volume have been very carefully executed by Messrs. A. and W. Dawson, and are as nearly as possible free from these defects. The process includes both photography and electrotype, but I am not able to give the reader very precise information as to the means by which the hollows are produced. The line, of course, is in relief, and always very nearly at the same level, as in woodcut.

The processes of photographic engraving have rendered very great services, especially to students of moderate means who live at a distance from great national collections, but the right use of reproductions must always be accompanied by a certain reserve. You can never trust them absolutely, for you can never be certain that a publisher will be a sufficiently severe critic to reject everything that is less than the best. They are most precious as memoranda of works that we have seen and know, and then the only limit to their usefulness is the danger that the reproduction which we possess may gradually take the place in our minds once occupied by the original which is absent.

*   *   *   *   *

Importance of Material Conditions in the Graphic Arts.

Technical studies have been so generally undervalued that the purpose of a book like this may be readily misunderstood or misrepresented. It may be supposed to deal with matter only, and to neglect the mental element in art, because it is not disdainful of material things. This would be a wrong estimate of its purposes.

In the Graphic Arts you *cannot* get rid of matter. Every drawing is *in* a substance and *on* a substance. Every substance used in drawing has its own special and peculiar relations both to nature and to the human mind.

The distinction in the importance of material things between the Graphic Arts and literature deserves consideration because our literary habits of thought lead us wrong so easily when we apply them to the arts of design. All of us who are supposed to be educated people have been trained in the mental habits which are derived from the study of books, and these habits, as all artists and men of science are well aware, lead students to value words and ideas more than things, and produce in their minds a sort of contempt for matter, or at least for the knowledge of matter, which indisposes them for material studies of all kinds, and often makes them blind to the close connexion which exists between matter and the artistic expression of thought.

In literature, such a connexion can scarcely be said to exist. A writer of books may use pen or pencil, and whatever quality of paper he chooses. There is even no advantage in reading the original manuscript, for the mechanical work of the printer adds clearness to the text without injuring the most delicate shades of literary expression. The quality of paper used by Sir Walter Scott did not affect one of his sentences; the quality of the different papers which were carefully selected by Turner, for studies of different classes, determined the kind of work he did upon them. Ink and pencil in the hands of a writer express exactly the same ideas; in the hands of a draughtsman they express different ideas or different mental conditions. A draughtsman does not interpret the light and shade of Nature in the same manner with different instruments. He has to throw himself into a temper which may be in harmony with the instrument he uses, to be blind for the time to the qualities it cannot render, to be sensitive to those which it interprets readily. Even the roughness or smoothness of the substance he is working upon determines many a mental choice.

Of these things a literary education gives us no perception. It even misleads our judgment by inducing us to suppose that substances are beneath the consideration of an artist, as they are outside the preoccupations of an author. Or it may falsify our opinions in another and more plausible way. It may, and it often does, induce people to think that technical matters may concern artists and still be below the region of the higher criticism which should interest itself in the things of the mind, and not bestow attention upon the products of the laboratory, or the processes of the painting-room. As a result of this way of thinking we sometimes hear critics praised for not being technical, and blunders in technical matters, which surprise those who understand the subject, do not appear to diminish the popularity of writers upon art, if only their style be elegant and their descriptions lively and amusing. Technical ignorance appears even to be an advantage to a critic, as it preserves him from one of the forms of tiresomeness, and leaves him to speak of sentiments which all can enter into rather than of substances which only workmen and students ever touch, and of processes which only the initiated can follow.

It will be my purpose in the present volume to show how mental expression is affected by material conditions in the graphic arts. I shall point out, not in vague generalities, but in accurate detail, the temptations offered by each substance used and each process employed. I shall make it clear in what manner, and to what degree, the artist has to conform himself to material conditions in order that he may best express the thoughts and sentiments which are in him, and, above all, I shall make it my business to show how the choice amongst those thoughts and sentiments themselves, how the expression of some and the suppression of others, may in very many instances be accounted for by the nature of the materials employed. It is only by a thorough understanding of these conditions of things that criticism can lay its foundations in truth and justice. You may write brilliantly about an artist without knowing anything of the inexorable material conditions under which his daily labour has to be done; you may captivate readers as disdainful of those conditions as yourself by the cleverness with which you can substitute rhetoric for information; but if you have any real desire to understand the fine arts as they are—if you have any keen intellectual curiosity about them, if you wish to speak with fairness of those who have worked in them—you will be brought to the study of matter as well as to the comparison of ideals. The criticism which professes indifference to technical knowledge is a criticism without foundations, however prettily it may be expressed. It is to the true criticism what a cloud is to a mountain—the one a changeful vapour sometimes gorgeous with transient colour and bearing a deceptive appearance of permanent form, the other massive and enduring, with a firm front to every wind and a base of granite deep-rooted in the very substance of the world.

There is a prevalent idea that the study of material conditions is uninteresting—a dull study, not fit to occupy the attention of highly cultivated persons. This idea comes from our curiously unsubstantial education. The training of a gentleman has been so much confined to words and mathematical abstractions that he has seldom learned to know the intimate charm which dwells in substances perfectly adapted to human purposes. There is a charm in things, in the mere varieties of matter, which affects our feelings with an exquisite sense of pleasurable satisfaction when we thoroughly understand the relations of these substances to the conceptions and creations of the mind.

Maxime Lalanne

A Treatise on Etching

1880. pp. 3-8

Definition and Character of Etching.

1. Definition.—An etching is a design fixed on metal by the action of an acid. The art of etching consists, in the first place, in drawing, with a *point* or *needle*, upon a metal plate, which is perfectly polished, and covered with a layer of varnish, or ground, blackened by smoke; and, secondly, in exposing the plate, when the drawing is finished, to the action of nitric acid. The acid, which does not affect fatty substances but corrodes metal, eats into the lines which have been laid bare by the needle, and thus the drawing is *bitten in*. The varnish is then removed by washing the plate with spirits of turpentine, and the design will be found to be engraved, as it were, on the plate. But, as the colour of the copper is misleading, it is impossible to judge properly of the quality of the work done until a *proof* has been taken.

2. Knowledge needed by the Etcher.—The aspirant in the art of etching, having familiarized himself by a few trials with the apperance of the bright lines produced by the needle on the dark ground of smoked varnish, will soon go to work on his plate confidently and unhesitatingly; and, without troubling himself much about the uniform appearance of his work, he will gradually learn to calculate in advance the conversion of his lines into lines more or less deeply bitten, and the change in appearance which these lines undergo when transferred to paper by means of ink and press.

It follows from this that the etcher must, from the very beginning of his work, have a clear conception of the idea he intends to realize upon his plate, as the work of the needle must harmonize with the character of the subject, and as the effect produced is finally determined by the combination of this work with that of the acid.

The knowledge needed to bring about these intimate relations between the needle, which produces the *drawing*, and the biting-in, which supplies the *color*, constitutes the whole science of the etcher.

3. Manner of Using the Needle.—Character of Lines.—The needle or point must be allowed to play lightly on the varnish, so as to permit the hand to move with that unconcern which is necessary to great freedom of execution. The use of a moderately sharp needle will insure lines which are full and nourished in the delicate as well as in the vigorous parts of the work. We shall thus secure the means of being simple. Nor will it be necessary to depart from this character even in plates requiring the most minute execution; all that is required will be a finer point, and lines of a more delicate kind. But the spaces left between the latter will be proportionately the same, or perhaps even somewhat wider, so as to prevent the acid from confusing the lines by eating away the ridges of metal which are left standing between the furrows. Freshness and neatness depend on these conditions in small as well as in large plates.

4. Freedom of Execution.—It is a well-known fact that the engraver who employs the burin (or graver), produces lines on the naked copper or steel which cross one another, and are measured and regular. It is a necessary consequence of the importance of line-engraving, growing out of its application to classical works of high style, that it should always show the severity and coldness of positive and almost mathematical workmanship. With etching this is not the case: the point must be free and capricious; it must accentuate the forms of objects without stiffness or dryness, and must delicately bring out the various distances, without following any other law than that of a picturesque harmony in the execution. It may be made to work with precision, whenever that is needed, but only to be abandoned afterwards to its

A TREATISE

ON

ETCHING.

TEXT AND PLATES

BY

MAXIME LALANNE.

AUTHORIZED AMERICAN EDITION, TRANSLATED FROM
THE SECOND FRENCH EDITION

BY

S. R. KOEHLER

WITH AN INTRODUCTORY CHAPTER AND NOTES BY THE
TRANSLATOR.

LONDON
W. & G. FOYLE LTD.
121-125 CHARING CROSS ROAD, W.C.2

natural grace. It will be well, however, to avoid over-excitement and violence in execution, which give an air of slovenliness to that which ought to be simply a revery.

5. How to produce Difference in Texture.—The manner of execution to be selected must conform to the nature of the objects. This is essential, as we have at our disposition only a point, the play of which on the varnish is always the same. It follows that we must vary its strokes, so as to make it express difference in texture. If we examine the etchings of the old masters, we shall find that they had a special way of expressing foliage, earth, rocks, water, the sky, figures, architecture, &c., without, however, making themselves the slaves of too constraining a tradition.

6. The Work of the Acid.—After the subject has been drawn on the ground, the acid steps in to give variety to the forms which were laid out for it by the needle, to impart vibration to this work of uniform aspect, and to inform it with the all-pervading warmth of life. In principle, a single biting ought to be sufficient; but if the artist desires to secure greater variety in the result by a succession of partial bitings, the different distances may be made to detach themselves from one another by covering up with varnish the parts sufficiently bitten each time the plate is withdrawn from the bath. The different parts which the mordant is to play must be regulated by the feeling: discreet and prudent, it will impart delicacy to the tender values; controlled in its subtle functions, it will carefully mark the relative tones of the various distances; less restrained and used more incisively, it will dig into the accentuated parts and will give them force.

7. The Use of the Dry Point.—If harmony has not been sufficiently attained, the *dry point* is used on the bare metal, to modify the values incompletely rendered, or expressed too harshly. Its office is to cover such insufficient passages with a delicate tint, and to serve, as Charles Blanc has very well expressed it, as a *glaze* in engraving.

8. Spirit in which the Etcher must work.—Follow your

feeling, combine your modes of expression, establish points of comparison, and adopt from among the practical means at command (which depend on the effect, and on which the effect depends) those which will best render the effect desired: this is the course to be followed by the etcher. There is plenty of the instinctive which practice will develop in him, and in this he will find a growing charm and an irresistible attraction. What happy effects, what surprises, what unforeseen discoveries, when the varnish is removed from the plate! A bit of good luck and of inspiration often does more than a methodical rule, whether we are engaged on subjects of our own invention,—*capricci*, as the Italians call them,— or whether we are drawing from nature directly on the copper. The great aim is to arrive at the first onset at the realization of our ideas as they are present in our mind. An etching must be virginal, like an improvisation.

9. Expression of Individuality in Etching.—Having once mastered the processes, the designer or painter need only carry his own individuality into a species of work which will no longer be strange to him, there to find again the expression of the talent which he displayed in another field of art. He will comprehend that etching has this essentially vital element, —and in it lies the strength of its past and the guaranty of its future,—that, more than any other kind of engraving on metal, it bears the imprint of the character of the artist. It personifies and represents him so well, it identifies itself so closely with his idea, that it often seems on the point of annihilating itself as a process in favor of this idea. Rembrandt furnishes a striking example of this: by the inter-mixture and diversity of the methods employed by him, he arrived at a suavity of expression which may be called magical; he diffused grace and depth throughout his work. In some of his plates the processes lend themselves so marvellously to the severest requirements of modelling, and attain such an extreme limit of delicacy, that the eye can no longer follow them, thus leaving the completest enjoyment to the intellect alone.

Claude Lorraine, on the other hand, knew how to conciliate freedom of execution with majesty of style.

10. **Value of Etching to Artists.**—Speaking of this subordination of processes in etching to feeling, I am induced to point out how many of the masters of our time, judging by the character of their work, might have added to their merits had they but substituted the etcher's needle for the crayon. Was not Decamps, who handled the point but little, an etcher in his drawings and his lithographs? Ingres only executed one solitary etching and yet, simply by virtue of his great knowledge, it seems as if in it he had given a presentiment of all the secrets of the craft. And did not Gigoux give us a foretaste of the work of the acid, when he produced the illustrations to his "Gil Blas," conceived in the spirit of an etcher, which, after thirty years of innumerable similar productions, are still the *chef-d'oeuvre* and the model of engraving on wood. And would Mouilleron have been inferior, if from the stone he had passed to the copper plate? It would be an easy matter to multiply examples chosen from among the artists who have boldly handled the needle, or from among those who might have taken it up with equal advantage, to prove that etching is not, as it has been called, a secondary method. There are no secondary methods for the manifestation of genius.

11. **Versatility of Etching.**—The needle is the crayon; the acid adds color. The needle is sometimes all the more eloquent because its means of expression are confined within more restricted limits. It is familiar and lively in the sketch, which by a very little must say a great deal; the sketch is the spontaneous letter. It all but reaches the highest expression when it is called in to translate a grand spectacle, or one of those fugitive effects of light which nature seems to produce but sparingly, so as to leave to art the merit of fixing them.

12. **Etching compared to other Styles of Engraving.**—By its very character of freedom, by the intimate and rapid connection which it establishes between the hand and the thoughts

of the artist, etching becomes the frankest and most natural of interpreters. These are the qualities which make it an honor to art, of which it is a glorious branch. All other styles of engraving can never be any thing but a means of reproduction. We must admire the knowledge, the intelligence, and the self-denial which the line-engraver devotes to the service of his art. But, after all, it is merely the art of assimilating an idea which is foreign to him, and of which he is the slave. By him the *chefs-d'oeuvre* of the masters are multiplied and disseminated, and sometimes, in giving eternity to an original work, he immortalizes his own name; but the part he has assumed inevitably excludes him from all creative activity.

13. Etching as a Reproductive Art.—These reserves having been made in regard to the engraver, whose instrument is the burin, justice requires that the reproductive etcher should come in for his proportional share, and that his functions should be defined. Some years ago, a school of etchers arose among us, whose mission it is to interpret those works of the brush which, by the delicacy and elegance of their character, cannot be harmonized with the severity of the burin. This school, to which Mr. Gaucherel gave a great impulse, has been called in to fill a regrettable void in the collections of amateurs. Every one knows those remarkable publications, *Les artistes contemporains*, and *Les peintres vivants*, which for the last twenty years, have reproduced in lithography the *chefs-d'oeuvre* of our exhibitions of paintings. To-day etching takes the place of lithography; it excels in the reproduction of modern landscapes, and of the *genre* subjects which we owe to our most esteemed painters. It is not less happy in the interpretation of certain of the old masters, whose works make it impossible to approach them with the burin. The catalogues of celebrated galleries which have lately been sold also testify to the important services rendered to art by the reproductive etcher. His methods are free and rapid; they are not subjected to a severe convention of form. He may rest his own work on the genius of others, so as to attain a success like that of the painter-etcher; but the latter, as he bathes his inspiration in the acid and triumphantly withdraws it, finds his power and his resources within himself alone. He is at once the translator and the poet.

Herbert Denison

A Treatise on Photogravure in Intaglio by the Talbot-Klič Process

1895. pp. 9-18

Introductory.

A photogravure plate is one of metal, preferably of copper, which bears on its surface in intaglio an etched representation of the subject to be reproduced. In other words, the portions of the plate representing the shadows and half-tones of the subject are sunk, instead of being the highest points—as in the case of half-tone and other blocks intended for use in ordinary letterpress printing—and the portions representing the high lights of the subject still retain the original level and surface of the plate.

This intaglio state of the plate is the result of the action of a mordant or etching fluid upon the metal, whereby the latter is etched or eaten away wherever the mordant comes in contact with it.

As the name given to the process indicates, in photogravure the etching of the metal is controlled by photographic means, and the process is therefore a mechanical one, to some extent at least, as distinguished from an "etching," properly so-called, and, because of its more or less mechanical nature, photogravure has been severely decried by the supporters of other intaglio methods of producing pictures.

With regard to original work, a print from a photogravure plate is open to the same criticism as a print direct from the negative, which is its foundation; and this, notwithstanding that the former is widely separated in its characteristics from a print by any purely photographic process. But it appears only reasonable to contend that in passing judgment on a picture the method of its production should be left entirely out of consideration, and that the visible result, and that only, should be regarded. After all, the true value of a picture is as a means of decoration, and the fact that in a photographic picture use has been made of the action of light should not detract from its value any more than does the fact that a painter also avails himself of the resources of nature in using the pigments that go to make his picture.

In the reproduction of paintings and drawings, however, photogravure stands on a different footing. The object here is to produce the most truthful and accurate reproduction possible of the original. As to accuracy of outline, there can be no serious contention that the engraver surpasses the lens; and in interpretation, photogravure has a distinct advantage over the engraver, in employing half-tone, instead of line, to reproduce a half-tone picture; and if photography is not yet quite equal to rendering with absolute truth the entire range of colours found in a picture, this difficulty can be overcome by handwork on the negative, supplemented by corrections on the copper.

The mechanical nature of photogravure is distinctly in its favour for reproductive purposes; there is no opportunity for the individuality of the engraver to leave an impress on the print antagonistic to that of the painter. It is the work of the painter in its entirety that the reproduction should portray —not a portion only of his work contaminated with the style and mannerisms of another, in whom, possibly, the possessor of the reproduction has no interest. The great increase within recent years in the number of photogravure reproductions of pictures proves that these advantages are appreciated by painter-artists.

It will probably lead to a better understanding of the photogravure process if the essentials common to plates by that process and to all intaglio plates are first considered, with the assistance of an outline of the methods of production of the chief varieties of such plates. These are three, namely—engravings, etchings, and mezzotints.

An engraving, as distinguished from an etching (for the term equally applies to an etching in so far as the image is in both varieties *engraven* on the metal by removal of a portion of its surface), is produced by the removal or digging out of portions of the metal—whether copper or steel—in lines or dots (stipple). The tool employed is a burin, consisting of a thin steel rod fastened into a wooden handle, round in shape, but with a flattened side, the cutting end of the tool being ground off flat at an angle of about 40°. With the handle held in the palm, the flat side being downwards, the burin is pushed along the plate, ploughing its way through and removing the metal in its progress.

The result is governed by the form of the incision, whether straight or curved, its depth, and the proximity of one line or dot to another. The shape of the incision can be further varied by the use of burins made from steel rods of different sections.

An etching differs from an engraving in that the removal of the metal is the result of the corrosive action of a mordant in place of the mechanical action of the burin. The plate is entirely covered with an "etching ground," impervious to acids, composed of wax with certain ingredients added to render it less brittle. The subject is then drawn upon the plate with needles of varying fineness, which, in their transit, remove the etching ground, and so lay bare the metal to the action of the mordant.

When the drawing is complete the plate is immersed in a

weak etching bath, composed of an acid diluted with water, and as the etching proceeds the plate is removed from time to time, rinsed and dried, and then the portions which have been sufficiently bitten are stopped out with varnish. This done, the plate is re-immersed, and the etching proceeds until it is necessary again to stop out, and so on until the darkest lines are sufficiently deep. The wax is then removed, and the plate is ready to be printed from.

Mezzotint engravings differ considerably from the foregoing varieties. The plate is first roughened over its entire surface by being rocked to and fro in various directions with a steel tool somewhat resembling the rocker of a cradle in appearance, and having its convex edge serrated. These saw-like teeth on the edge of the rocker indent the plate, and as the metal is not removed, but displaced only, it rises slightly round each indentation, thus increasing its depth, and producing what is known technically as a "burr."

A plate, if properly rocked, would, if printed at this stage, yield a perfectly black impression. The picture is produced by removing with a scraper both burr and indentations where the whites of the subject are to be, removing them partially only, and to a greater or less degree for the half-tones, and leaving the plate untouched in the darkest portions of the picture.

From subsequent descriptions, it will be seen that a mezzotint plate more closely resembles one produced by photogravure than either of the others previously described.

In the case of all intaglio plates, the method of printing is by filling the depressions with a stiff fatty ink of a special nature, and afterwards removing the ink from the surface only by means of muslins of different qualities, the final polish to the high lights being given by the hand.

The plate is laid on the iron bed of a copper-plate press, a piece of plate paper quite limp with moisture is placed on the top, with three or four pieces of blanketing on the paper, and the whole is passed through the rollers. The pressure, aided by the yielding nature of the blanket, forces the paper into the depressions of the plate where it comes into contact with the ink, and on raising the paper from the plate, the former will be found to have licked up the ink, and retained it on its surface. The paper and ink together in reality form a cast of the subject depicted on the plate.

From this brief outline (the subject of printing will be more fully dealt with hereafter) it will be readily understood that in order that the ink, in the process of cleaning the surface or "wiping," may not be removed from the depressions as well as the surface of the plate, it is essential that it should be confined in spaces not so large as to permit of the muslin sinking into them during its passage over the plate. In etchings and engravings this confinement of the ink is natural, consequent upon the subject being expressed in line or stipple, the only thing to avoid being the running together of lines placed close together, due in etchings to the lateral action of the mordant; while in mezzotint engravings the same result is attained by the roughening of the plate, the rocker producing a cellular surface eminently suited to the retention of ink.

The etching of a plate in pure half-tone (say a photograph from nature), in which the tones gradually merge one into another frequently without any perceptible step between, and where almost the entire picture is etched to some extent, would not yield a surface with this retentive quality sufficiently pronounced to truthfully render the tones of the subject. A magnified section of such a plate would simply show an undulation of surface corresponding to the depth to which the etching had been carried. It will be seen from the accompanying sketch of a section of such a plate (fig. 1) that there would be nothing to prevent the ink being removed in the process of wiping from the whole of the etched portions of the image, except under the shoulders formed by the margins and by small patches of high-light at various points of the subject. This difficulty was met with by all the early workers, who found that, although the roughness of the

Fig. 1.
AA The original surface level of the plate.
B The etched portion.

metal resulting from the action of the mordant enabled light tones to be rendered correctly, it was insufficient to retain the necessary amount of ink to produce dark tones.

The difficulty was to some extent surmounted by Fox Talbot, by applying a resinous dust to the surface of the gelatine resist; but this was in connection with the process in which the plate to be engraved is coated with the bichromatised gelatine, exposed behind the transparency, and etched without washing out the soluble gelatine.

It is to Klič that we are indebted for the idea of protecting the metal, before the transfer thereto of the resist, by an acid-resisting gum distributed evenly over its surface in the form of fine particles, which are caused to adhere to the plate by heat. This ground, while protecting the metal, also afforded a surface which would retain in position a gelatine resist produced by the carbon process, and transferred to the plate for development. Prior to this, the carbon process could not be used because the resist invariably stripped off the bright metal on drying.

The effect of the grain obtained in this way (fig. 2) is to break up the comparatively large depression, representing a flat tone in the subject, into a multitude of minute depressions or cells, each of which is divided from its neighbours by small patches or points of somewhat pyramidal form, having their bases at a depth from the surface proportionate to the darkness of tone to be reproduced, and their apices being the

Fig. 2.
AA The original surface level of the plate.
B The etched portion protected by the ground.

original surface of the metal. The surface of the plate, after etching, will partake somewhat of the nature of a fine file, and will be found to retain the ink in its various parts exactly in proportion to the depth of the cells.

Charles G. Harper

A Practical Handbook of Drawing for Modern Methods of Reproduction

1894. pp. 41-47

Examples will now be shown of the varying results obtainable from the same drawings by different processes.

The drawing representing a *Misty Day at Bolt Head* was made upon common rough paper, such as is usually found in sailors' log-books; in fact, it was a log-book the present writer used during the greater part of a tour in Devon, nothing else being obtainable in those parts save the cloth-bound, gold-lettered sketch-books whose porterage convicts one at once of amateurishness. And here let me say that a sailor's log-book, though decidedly an unconventional medium for sketching in, seems to be entirely admirable. The paper takes pencil excellently well, and the faint blue parallel lines with which the pages are ruled need bother no one; they will not (being blue) reproduce. To save the freshness of the impression, the sketch was lightly finished in ink, and sent for reproduction uncleaned. The illustration shows the result. It is an example of the bitumen process, whose original sin of exaggerating all the pencil marks which it has been good enough to reproduce at all is partly cloaked by the intervention of

Pen and pencil drawing, reproduced by bitumen process.

Pen and pencil drawing, reproduced by swelled gelatine process.

hand-work all over the block. You can see how continually the graver has been put through the lines to produce a greyness, yet how unsatisfactory the result!

The drawing was now sent for reproduction by the swelled gelatine process. The result is a much more satisfactory block. Everything that the original contained has been reproduced. The sullen blacknesses of the pinnacled rocks are nothing extenuated, as they were in the first example, where they seem comparatively insignificant and the technical qualities of pen and pencil are retained throughout, and can readily be identified. The same remarks apply even more strongly to the small blocks from the *Note at Gorran*.

But such a pure pen-drawing as that of *Charlwood*, shown [p. 196] in blocks by (1) Messrs. Dawson's swelled gelatine process, and (2) by Mr. Chefdeville's sympathetic handling of the albumen process, would have come almost equally well by bitumen, or by an ordinary practitioner's treatment of albumen. It offered no technical difficulties, and there is exceedingly little to choose between these two blocks. Careful examination would show that a very slight thickening of line had taken place throughout the block by the gelatine method, and this must ever be the distinguishing difference between that process and those in which acids are used to eat away the metal of the block—that the gelatine renders at its best every jot and tittle of a drawing, and would by the nature of the process rather exaggerate than diminish; and that in those processes in which acids play a part, the processman must be ever watchful lest his zinc plate be "overetched"—lest the upstanding metal lines be eaten away to a scratchy travesty of the original drawing. But you will see that although the lines in the swelled gelatine *Charlwood* are appreciably thicker than in its albumen fellow, yet the latter prints darker. The explanation is in the metals of which the two blocks are composed. Zinc prints more heavily than copper.

A Note at Gorran
Pen and pencil drawing, reproduced by bitumen process.

A Note at Gorran
Pen and pencil drawing, reproduced by swelled gelatine process.

Pen-drawing reproduced by swelled gelatine process.

Pen-drawing reproduced by Chefdeville.

Joseph Pennell

Pen Drawing and Pen Draughtsmen
1894. pp. 41-42, 445-450

Daniel Vierge

As Menzel is responsible for the development of pen drawing in Germany and England, so is Vierge for the present style and the great advance in technique of draughtsmen in France, Italy, Spain, and America. I know that Vierge falls apparently under Sir Joshua Reynolds' condemnation of superificial cleverness. But when a man draws with Vierge's knowledge and adds to it his skill in handling, his work is something vastly more than clever, although every line might seem to deserve this condemnation. Because Vierge is followed by a number of men in France, Italy, Spain, and America, who, if they lack a certain amount of his inventive cleverness, have added to it much that is original of their own,—although I admit they would never have worked after his manner had he not led the way,—a certain number of critics, and artists too, jump to the conclusion that anybody can do this sort of work. Yet the fact remains that the number of these clever men has not increased, nor have any other draughtsmen been able to supersede them. They in their turn have had their imitators, men without the slightest knowledge of the means used by Vierge to obtain his effects, but no one, even among Vierge's immediate followers, has yet succeeded in surpassing him.

Vierge doubtless owed much to Fortuny and much to Gigoux, that early and little-known Frenchman of this century. The greater part of his work, and certainly the most characteristic, is done with pen and ink, and, like Fortuny, he uses the pen to fill his drawings with delicate modelling. But however much he learned from his great countryman, he brought to his work a strength, a delicacy, and a character

that were all his own. From the beginning there was no mistaking it for that of any other draughtsman. Not that it is in the least mannered; in looking over the pages of *Pablo de Ségovie* one is struck with the entirely different methods used in the many drawings. With this cleverness of technique one finds the most perfect modelling in the tiniest figures and faces, the most artistic rendering of architecture, the most graceful suggestions of landscape; and the assured touch of the master stamps each and every drawing with individuality.

To get the refinement given in the beautiful little cuts from *Pablo de Ségovie*, it is necessary to make one's drawings very large and yet at the same time to work with the greatest amount of delicacy. There is next to no cross-hatching except in Vierge's later work done since his illness, and therefore his drawings can be reduced to almost any extent without the lines filling up. Still, in the volume of *Pablo de Ségovie*, the blocks were almost too small to do full justice to his work, as any one can see by comparing them with the larger reproductions here given. Then, again, when he wishes to get a rich colour, he uses a positive black, in the reproduction of which there is apparently no change, although it is a perfectly well-known fact that the whites of any reproduction

grow whiter and the blacks blacker as the size decreases.
Another quality to be noted in his work is the amount of
colour suggested without the use of it. Many of Vierge's
later drawings are marred by the introduction of large splotches
of pure black—neither put in with a feeling for decorative
balance nor colour effect. This can be most plainly and
unfortunately seen in the English edition of *Pablo*. Again,
too, he has used tint backgrounds, and Vierge himself ordered
them to be used and not the photo-engraver, as some of his
would-be critics and exploiters assert.

There is really very little to be said about Vierge's drawings, except to advise the student to study them in the most thorough manner, and to remind him that their cleverness and apparent freedom are the result of years of the hardest study, and, in each drawing, of days and sometimes weeks of the most careful work. After all I have said, it is almost useless for me to repeat that the effects of light and shade in Vierge's designs, being intended for Spanish or southern subjects, are of course utterly out of keeping in drawings made in England. But the cleverness, the skill, is never out of keeping, and the nearer it can be approached, the better for the pen draughtsman and the art of pen drawing.

* * * * *

Hopes and Fears for Pen Drawing

I have tried to show what pen drawing is, and in conclusion I should like to state my great hopes, and greater fears, for the future of the art. I have already pointed out that pen drawing is supposed to be despised by almost everybody but a few artists and art editors, some of the latter having given it recognition simply because of its cheapness for reproduction. I hope therefore to see an art, which is looked down upon to-day by the same people who despised etching until Mr. Hamerton opened their eyes to its true value, put in its proper place—that is, in equal rank with etching.

A good etching is only a successful pen drawing after all. The qualities of softness, richness, and mistiness can be given by a master of pen drawing, and reproduced in photogravure so cleverly, as to deceive the most accomplished art critic. Smudges, accidental foul biting, and a thousand other things that go to make the value of the state of an etching by Whistler, Haden, or Méryon, can be obtained in ten minutes by a clever man with an old tooth brush and a rough-skinned thumb, while the drawing, the only autographic and valuable part of the production, is exactly the same, and the tone, the softness, and effect of any unwiped plate can be produced by a good printer for a few pence extra. It is really for blemishes and defects, accidental or intentional on the part of the very thoughtful artist, that the collector prizes its rare first state. The value attached to the print from an etched plate is fictitious; the value of a pen drawing is real. The pen drawing is the artist's work; the etching is only a print from it, often not satisfactory to the artist, for though he sees just what he wants on the copper-plate, neither he nor the printer can get it from the plate to the paper. With the etching, as with the pen drawing, there is only one person who can own the original. A print from a photogravure of a pen drawing is really of as much value as the print from an etching. The only difference is that in nine cases out of ten the etching is a failure, the photogravure a success. The collector may own the single pen drawing, but he hardly every troubles himself to buy the original copper-plate which is owned by the dealer, and which—and not the print from it—is the real equivalent to the pen drawing. But so ignorant are some amateurs and collectors that they pay high prices for artists' proofs of photogravures and autotypes, which cannot even boast of rarity, and are only better than prints inasmuch as an early pull of any plate is of course sharper and clearer, and therefore better, than a later one. I have heard the intelligent collector persuaded into paying £20 for an etching which was quite without artistic merit, and which in a few years will sell for 20s; while, for a guinea or so more, he had a gorgeous frame thrown in, which, he was assured, he only got at that price because all the other subscribers were having exactly the same thing!

To value a work of art only for its rarity is a feeling with which I have no sympathy. But it is strange that collectors should not see that an original drawing which they can own and preserve, and which need not be duplicated if they do not wish it, is of more value according to their own standard than a print, which five hundred or fifty thousand other people can own, and over which they have no control. They are in fact influenced by dealers who publish almost all the etchings, and are not willing to encourage the work which would bring them comparatively small profit.

In a recent conversation with a dealer, he admitted my facts to be perfectly true, but in the next breath he said he would fight against them so long as he continued in the print business. For the simple reason that he could purchase an etched plate for the same amount of money he would have to pay for a good pen drawing; that if the plate proved popular, he could sell thousands of proofs from it, some of which, containing cabalistic and inartistic scrawls, would bring ten times more than others which only contained the artist's signature, while these would sell for twice as much as the ordinary plain prints; the plain prints themselves being probably quite as good as the first pulls from the plate, because the artist now steels his plate the moment it is finished. Exactly the same result could be obtained by the dealer buying a pen drawing, having a photogravure made from it and selling the prints. I know that this result is to be had with absolute certainty, while every etching ordered by a dealer is an uncertain speculation. Still, if dealers would go to the leading pen draughtsmen of the day, they would be as sure to get good drawings as they are now certain of getting bad etchings from artless etchers. All that is needed is a little exploiting, but dealers will never do this for themselves. For all business—and etching is no longer an art, but only a business and a trade—is conducted on the most short-sighted principles —principles which are rapidly running it into the ground. But until nothing more can be made from etchings, though the market is flooded with them, dealers will refuse to turn their attention to anything else. I know, as I have said, that if pen drawing can be made to seem worth the financial attention of dealers, the result will be, mainly, more money in their pockets. But still, with so many good pen draughtsmen now at work, it may show the public that there is at the present moment a healthy, flourishing art. However, somebody must compel the dealers to take up pen drawing, if it is to be taken up by them at all, for they will never do so of themselves.

The objection most art editors find to pen drawing is, that it is not understood by the masses. I have made many pen drawings, not only in the house, but among the people, and I have heard from them more expressions of pleasure in a pen drawing, both while it was being made and after it was finished, than I have ever heard given to a pencil or a wash drawing. The reason is easy to explain. In pen drawing the details, the windows of houses, the delicacy of trees or the study of a figure half an inch high, are all worked out carefully, lovingly, and artistically, while in wash drawings these details may be only suggested, and to the average mortal artistic suggestion is absolutely meaningless.

That children like pen drawings needs no proof. The success of Randolph Caldecott's, Kate Greenaway's, Adrien Marie's, and Reginald Birch's drawings,—whether they have a slight wash of colour or not is of no consequence,—answers all arguments to the contrary. Of course, as the educated child grows up, its innate ideas of art are so quickly suppressed that in the end bad drawings are not infrequently preferred to good. It is only wonderful that any one cares in the least for drawing.

That some people do, however, is proved by the popularity of magazines like the *Century* and *Harper's*, and of illustrated weeklies like *Le monde illustré* and *Fliegende Blätter*. As far as I know, the utterly inartistic and pseudo-comic papers, which are usually illustrated by pen drawings, have the largest circulation of any illustrated English periodicals—*Ally Sloper's Half-Holiday*, for example, though I ought to add that, technically, the late Mr. Baxter's rendering of Ally Sloper was excessively clever.

Newspapers which really appeal to the masses, and in which there is never mention of the word art, are beginning to use pen drawings, some of which are not bad, though the majority are atrocious. A few of the portraits and little sketches that have appeared in the *Pall Mall Gazette* are good, but frequently they have been remarkable only for their artlessness. But it is in newspapers that my greatest hopes and fears for the future of pen drawing lie. I hope that some great inventor like Walter or Hoe may turn his attention —as I believe he will—to artistic newspaper printing. If he does he will kill every magazine. For just as literary men are only too willing to work for the newspapers, so would the pen draughtsman be, if he could get his work well printed. And this would merely mean bringing art to the people, where we are told it was in Italy some hundreds of years ago. For just as the people are said to have gone to church to see their art, so many now seek for everything, art included, in the newspapers. But I fear that when this comes to pass, the second state of art will be worse than the first, unless the newspaper office is revolutionised and an art editor introduced. For the news editor would very likely accept whatever came to hand.

Not only can an illustrated newspaper be printed daily, but more than one is published to-day. The New York *Daily Graphic* and the Paris *Charivari* are examples. The last time I saw the New York *Graphic*, however, it was still suffering under the disadvantage of not having any good men to work for it. Instead of employing good artists, it was content with cheap-looking work, just as the average newspaper, instead of getting a staff of men whose writing would give literary value to its volumes, employs people whose special aim seems to be to write stupidly and to enlarge upon the power of journalism —*i.e.* of themselves. That their power is great, owing to the ignorance of the public, is unfortunately unquestionable. And for this reason, with the general use of drawings in papers, they would be able to bring art down to the same level to which they too frequently debase literature. In the illustrated daily of the future, the plan that will have to be pursued is this: all sorts of illustrated news must be reproduced by the Meisenbach or other process from photographs;

slight sketches could be made by clever men in three or four hours, and reproduced in time to appear in the next, or possibly the same, day's paper; more important work must be delayed several days or a week, but still the daily would be much ahead of the weeklies with its news.

My greatest fear is only that such a paper would be an instant and phenomenal success, and that its managers would make their fortunes and then, like those of other papers started by a brilliant set of young artists, engravers, and journalists, become merely stockholders, pocket the profits, and allow the paper to fall to a lower level than that of the publications it was going to improve. It is just this, one fears for pen drawing in every direction. The difficulty of keeping to a very high standard is shown in *L'Art* which has very noticeably gone down during the last few years. The only consolation is that pen drawing eventually ruins the people who use it by abusing it. *Our Continent*, an American publication, which started with the most brilliant prospects, was wrecked exactly from this cause; it began to publish nothing but poor pen drawings and quickly came to grief. Papers which do continue to improve week by week and month by month are the *Century, Harper's, Fliegende Blätter.* Unless there is an art editor who can draw to himself a clever staff of artists and keep them, an illustrated paper can neither go on, nor maintain the position it has reached.

There is an enormous demand for pen drawing growing daily, and though the supply apparently equals it, pen drawing as an art is not advancing. There are a few artists who really care for it in itself, and endeavour with each new drawing to make something of value, but outside of the larger magazines in which their work usually appears, they apparently make no impression on the majority of pen draughtsmen who are filling books and papers with artless drawings. Any one who will look back, especially through the European magazines and the *Century*, will see that some of the very best pen drawings were made between 1879 and

1883, before this vast army of scribblers had sprung up and found that their wretched work was of value to people as ignorant as themselves. Just as architects are wanted to restore or ruin whatever little beauty is left in the world, so this ever-increasing army of pen draughtsmen, one might think, is wanted to lower the standard of pen drawing and turn it farther and farther away from its legitimate end.

Because so many pen drawings are now made, it has been said that for artists who work in pen and ink "their only chance of relative immortality is a reputation won in some other department of art." A sufficient answer to this assertion is to be had in the drawings of four men—to mention no more,—Fortuny, Rico, Menzel, and Vierge, which will be known so long as there is any love for art. It might as well be said that because thousands of artless pictures are painted and exhibited every year, a good painter, in order to be remembered, must make his reputation as a sculptor or an architect.

Though it seems as if Mr. Hamerton and Mr. Haden have shown people the beauty and true province of etching, only to make the fortune of print-dealers and to set on pinnacles men who transgress every law governing etching as a fine art, yet at the same time, etchers like Whistler, Haden, and Buhot occasionally produce plates which prove the beauty and province of the art have not been entirely forgotten. In like manner there is a strong saving remnant among pen draughtsmen, and upon it hopes for the future of pen drawing can safely rest. But if good pen drawing is to be confined to these few men, and elsewhere to be used as a medium for disseminating the cheapest and worst art, the outlook is dark enough. Whether the few will leaven the whole is doubtful. But they certainly will never be swallowed up entirely, and their work, like all good art, will live.

Edmund J. Sullivan
***

The Art of Illustration
1921. pp. 184-188

Suggestions to be Found in Copper-plate Engraving for Pen Drawing

While the mediaevally inclined among book illustrators have been inspired by the work of the wood-cutter of line, since his work was designed to be printed in the same manner as letterpress, and frequently with it, there is as much or more reason why he should look, not to the wood-cutters but to the engravers on copper as exemplars of strict style, if he must look backwards for inspiration, since the burin naturally yields a line much more in correspondence with our modern steel nib than the line left by the wood-cutter's knife, and is equally reproducible. It has to be borne in mind always that the wood-cutter had to make two lines always to the draughtsman's one, and it is remarkable how well he generally managed to preserve the illusion that the draughtsman's line is the work of the wood-cutter, rather than the white space in which it exists. It is the white and not the black that is the wood-cutter's work, it being his business to see that the white should touch without impinging upon the black line drawn upon the wood by the artist. It is indeed miraculous with what fidelity his uninspiring task was carried out, since any display of personality on his own part, except in a capacity for devoted self-sacrifice, must prove a fatal impertinence. It remains none the less that the line printed from a wood block is not the wood-cutter's or wood engraver's line; it is the white spaces that are his handiwork, while the line of an engraver upon metal is the engraver's own, and corresponds more nearly to the characteristic stroke of a pen than that

Sandys. King War-Wolf. A noble drawing.
While maintaining Dürer's strictness of style, Sandys contrived to add
local colour and a fuller light and shade.

Sandys. Harald Harfagr. A magnificent example of combination
of strict line, light and shade, local colour, and tone.

which the wood-cutter has had ever so gingerly to approach and leave alone.

The modern pen draughtsman, therefore, in looking back, while not neglecting the great wood cuts as a basis for the formation of style in drawing, should not neglect a study of the engravings on metal of the same period. There is no reason why the virility of the one should not be combined with the delicacy of the other in due proportion, since modern methods of photographic reproduction can render either or both at once with impartial ease and fidelity, the only restraining considerations for the artist being the appropriateness of their employment, the quality of the paper, and the printing to be expected.

That any humane being can be found to regret the days of the facsimile wood engraver is a wonder, since here is a case where the hand is definitely inferior to the machine. Accuracy was the highest requirement, and it would be as unhumane to desire the mistress of the house with great pains to miscalculate the servants' wages for the month rather than to get them right by the simple means of a ready-reckoner. And yet many humane people do sigh for everything to be "hand done," instead of devoting their energies towards seeing that the machine is properly directed. The risk of the employment of a machine is that things are sometimes made so easy that a habit of entire carelessness is induced, and the machine is blamed for the defects of the man behind it.

The V shaped burin, if used with variations of force, ploughs a line more nearly resembling in its varying thickness that of the pen than does the etched line, and the work of a master of the burin might be studied as a corrective against any tendency towards sloppiness of style. Not being so facile of handling as the pen, economy, precision, and restraint are virtues which the burin imposes, where the pen sometimes runs away with the artist and leads to profusion, indefinition, and haphazard workmanship.

John Southward

*Progress in Printing and the Graphic Arts during the
Victorian Era*

1897. pp. 5-11, 32-43, 74-78

Progress in Jobbing Printing—Improvement in the Style of Ornamental Types—Taste in Display.

This cursory retrospect would have to be attempted in the spirit of the writer of the immortal treatise, "On Snakes in Ireland," if a dictum of the late Mr. William Morris could be accepted. That master of many arts declared that "no good printing had been done since 1550." Printing was at its zenith at the close of the first century of its existence. After then, no good printing, he said, was to be found.

I venture to protest against this view; and in the following pages hope to show that printing is by no means in a state of decadence. On the contrary, I will try to point out that very good printing is done. My contention is, in fact, that better printing has been done during the last sixty years—in each of the three principal branches of the business: job, news, and book printing—that was ever done before. To establish this it will only be necessary, I think, to contrast the workmanship, the appliances, the materials, of 1897 with those of 1837.

I begin with jobbing work, which might be regarded as the least important of the three branches of the printing business. Its products are more ephemeral than any others. A newspaper is often only read for half-an-hour, and is then thrown aside and forgotten. But the great bulk of jobbing work has a shorter life even than this. Much of it is instantly consigned to the waste-paper basket or the dust-heap. There is another peculiarity about it. It is not paid for by the person who is to become its possessor. We have to buy every other

MR. HORACE PORTER

IS at present personally engaged at Western Hall on large and important Photographic work, extending to the end of July, and while there he would be able to make any Photographs you may require, without charging for distance or travelling expenses.

SPECIMENS OF WORK AND ESTIMATES SUPPLIED.

Specialities: At Home Portraiture, Groups, Animals, Interiors and Exteriors.

Messrs. Pardonable & Pride, Western Street, W., say: "Your beautiful work is perfection itself."

HORACE PORTER.

SPECIALIST IN PHOTOGRAPHY,
864 BATTLE HILL, S.W.

Jobbing printing of the past.

kind of printing, but this is given away. We do not pay for the circulars thrust into our letter-boxes, or the invoices sent us by our tradesmen. Hence it might be thought that any kind of work and material would do for jobbing. As a matter of fact there is quite as much typographical skill expended on it as on bookwork. Again, its importance is shown by the preponderating number of persons constantly engaged in it—far more than in news and book-printing put together. Bookwork, as a special branch, is done in only two dozen towns throughout the kingdom; there is hardly a respectably-sized village without its jobbing printer. There are, perhaps, only about 2,000 newspaper printing establish-ments (for some of them do several different papers); there are at least 8,000 general jobbing offices.

The character of jobbing printing depends to a large extent upon the ornamental types used in it. Now, at the begin-ning of the present century there were no ornamental types of any kind; if display was required it had to be obtained by some novel disposition of plain romans, italics, or blacks. Not long before the Queen came to the throne, however, there arose a demand for something more ornate and decor-ative. The founders responded to this demand by providing

---

Mr. Horace Porter

Messrs.
Pardonable & Pride,
Western Street, W.,
say :
" Your beautiful work is
perfection itself."

Is at present personally engaged at Western Hall on large and important photographic work, extending to the end of July, and while there he would be able to make any photography you may require, without charging for distance or travelling expenses. ✳ ✳ ✳

Specimens of work and Estimates supplied.

SPECIALITIES :
At Home Portraiture.
Groups, Animals,
Interiors & Exteriors.

Horace Porter,

Specialist in ✒ ✒
Photography,

864 Battle Hill, S.W.

Jobbing work—style of the present day.

type styles which were copied mainly from the lettering of
the writing masters, imitating their absurd and inelegant
flourishes and pen-shading; from that of the painters who
"wrote" shop facias; and that of copper-plate engravers, who
often in engraving cards and book-plates combined the
eccentricities of the painters with the affectations of the
writing masters. The result was a style of type faces which
was simply execrable. Examples of them are given in these
pages. These letters expose an utter want of taste on the part
of their designers. This had its parallel in a want of taste on
the part of those who used the types. They thought that all
sorts of jobs should be set up in "monumental" style, which
was a combination of the style of lettering on a modern title
page and on a tombstone. Its leading feature is that lines
should be alternated in regard to length—a big line was to be
followed by a little one; and then a big one should come in,
and so on. Further, each of these lines should occupy the
middle of the measure of the composition; if it was short,
half the space must go before the line and half after it. The
specimens presented exhibit the system as then followed.
The long lines were said to be "full out," and the little ones
were the catch-lines. The supposed necessity for certain
lines to be "full out" led to the fashioning of some of the
most awkward letters imaginable. The principal line might
consist of only one word, which if set in a letter of normal
proportions would be too short. Hence outrageously "extended" letters were produced. If these were not sufficient to
fill up the measure, spaces were put between them. To meet
cases where the wording would not otherwise come into the
line, extremely attenuated or "condensed" letters were cut.
These very wide and very narrow letters were unsightly and
unreadable. It was another canon of bad taste never to set
a leading line in lower-case, although lower-case letters are
nearly always more legible a little distance off than capitals.

These rules prevailed up to within the last twenty years,
and no printer dared to contravene them. An altogether dif-

ferent style now prevails, and its existence marks a progress of the most decided and valuable character. The new style is characterised by freedom from conventional restraints; a commonsense and logical grouping of words; and the introduction, within due bounds, of appropriate ornamentation. It is recognised by the printers that excellence consists in making the composition attractive, and the object of its production—whether a card or a circular—apparent at a glance, in giving full prominence to prominent expressions; in refraining from making big lines merely because he possesses big type, and little ones because he has narrow type. He sees that there is really no reason, in the nature of things, why wording should be divided into centred lines like those of the tombstone. Instead of covering all the available space with lines needlessly long or needlessly large, he either leaves blanks, which contrast with the lettering and emphasise it, or fills up the vacant spaces with appropriate ornaments, which add to utility—beauty. Much more discrimination is now shown than at any previous period in the selection of type. The extravagantly ornate types are quite in disfavour. Purer and simpler styles are sought for; and more attention is paid to originality of treatment, symmetry and harmony, and general effectiveness.

Another decided mark of progress is shown in the greater use of colours than formerly, and of different kinds of colours. At the beginning of the reign the average printer possessed only two colours—red and blue. These were, as a rule, raw and gaudy. He obtained his chromatic effects—such as they were—by ringing the changes on these, with an admixture of black lines. Some printers had green and yellow, and these formed the limit of the typographical colour-box. The few colours were used with extravagance or with niggardliness, according to the price to be received for the job, and with little regard to appropriateness or harmony. For some years these primary colours have been nearly abandoned, except for admixture with others forming new and more

THE SCOTS LODGE

OF THE

Most Ancient and Honourable Fraternity of Free and Accepted Masons, No. 2319, England.

W. BRO. JOSEPH J. WHITEHEAD,

Worshipful Master.

BURNS

ANNIVERSARY

BANQUET.

ON

Thursday, the 23rd January, 1896,

AT

THE SCOTS CORPORATION HALL,

CRANE COURT, FLEET STREET,

LONDON.

Jobbing printing of the past.

urns &
Anniversary
Banquet. ❦❦

The : Scots : Lodge
of the ✿✿✿✿✿✿✿✿✿✿✿✿✿
Most Ancient and ❦❦❦❦
Honourable Fraternity of
Free and ✿✿✿✿✿✿✿✿✿✿✿
✿✿✿✿✿✿ Accepted Masons,
❦❦❦ No. 2319, England,
W. Bro. ✿✿✿✿✿✿✿✿✿✿✿
✿✿ Joseph J. Whitehead,
❦❦❦ Worshipful Master.

The Scots Corporation Hall,
Crane : Court : Fleet : St.
London : on : Thursday,
the : 23rd : January,
✿✿✿ 1896 ✿✿✿

Jobbing work—style of the present day.

subdued tints and art shades. Besides inks, dry colours are supplied which can be made into inks by the admixture with them of varnishes. There will be used such tints as rose, salmon, blue, citron-yellow, sea-green, buff, mauve, grey; in shades green-black, blue-black, and brown. The colour scheme for a circular may include chromotype-yellow, chromotype-red with equal part varnish, milori-blue and varnish, burnt umber, chocolate-brown, olive-green, black—all varieties of hues unattempted by the printer sixty years ago. He had not the colours; if he had possessed them he would not have had the taste or the skill to use them. Advances in art education largely account for this progress. The public have plainly shown a disposition to remunerate printers for doing more artistic work. The demand for it created the supply, and when printers called for the means of doing such work, the ink-makers bestirred themselves to provide what was wanted. We have not yet attained to the excellence in colour printing of some of our foreign rivals, but during the last few years we have undoubtedly made great advances.

*   *   *   *   *

The Power Press—Invention of Cylindrical Machine by Koenig —The Four-feeder "Times" Machine of Cowper and Applegath —The Applegath Upright Rotary—Hoe's Type-Revolving Press —The Walter Rotary Web Machine—Insetting and Supplement Machines—Multiple Web Machines—Speeds of Modern Machines —Apparatus for Bookwork and General Commercial Printing.

It has been mentioned that in 1837 nearly all printing was done on the hand press. For a few years previously, however, there had been in operation in the offices of some of the largest book printers and for printing journals having what was then considered very large circulations, not presses, but "machines." In these the principle of impression by platen, actuated by screws and levers, was abandoned, and instead of it there was used a revolving metal cylinder, to squeeze the paper on to the inked type forme. The first apparatus of the kind was constructed by Frederick Koenig, a German printer, who, while working at Leipzig was impressed with the idea

Frederick Koenig.

that the operations of printing might be simplified and accelerated. He received no encouragement in Germany, and came to London in 1806. Thomas Bensley, a well-known printer, provided him with funds to work out his scheme and two other extensive printers afterwards joined the partner-ship. In 1810 he produced a platen machine. As a printer, he could conceive of nothing better than modifying the methods with which he was accustomed. It will be seen, in this short sketch of advances made in the art of printing, that the really important improvements—the revolutionary ideas which have resulted in the marvels of the press of to-day— came almost without exception, from men who were not themselves practical and professional printers. Had they been printers, they would probably have projected nothing better than variations of the apparatus and methods to which they were accustomed. Some years before this a patent for an entirely novel kind of printing had been taken out by William Nicholson, a mechanic and scientific author, but not a printer by trade. He proposed to discard the platen in favour of a cylinder as the pressing surface. This was a project only, for Nicholson never really constructed a machine. Koenig no doubt had this specification brought under his notice. He then gave up the platen idea, and produced a machine in which Nicholson's principle of a cylinder was adopted. Two sheets of a book were printed on this machine in 1812. The remarkable character of the invention reaching the ears of Mr. John Walter, of the "Times," he went to see it, and forthwith ordered a machine to print his newspaper. This machine was completed in 1814, and on the 28th of November of that year a newspaper was for the first time printed by machinery, and by machinery driven by steam.

It was a double cylinder machine, which printed simul-taneously two copies of a forme of the newspaper on one side only. The feeding was done at the two ends; the inking was effected by providing a vertical cylinder with a hole at the bottom fitted with an air-tight piston, depressed by a screw, which forced the ink out on to two hard rollers, between which it was distributed, and from which it was furnished to the other rollers. The machine printed 1,800 impressions per hour.

The invention of a cylindrical machine, driven from a main shaft and impelled by motive power, was an event of importance second only to that of the invention of printing itself. All modern improvements have their basis in this rotatory apparatus. The hand press, with its nine separate processes involved in the printing of a single sheet could not be much accelerated in its operation. The machine, on the other hand, was subject to no such limitation of output. As will be shown presently, by increasing the number of pressing cylinders and the means of supplying it with paper its capabilities may be almost infinitely increased.

When, in course of time, it was found necessary to improve Koenig's machine, Mr. Walter called in Mr Edward Cowper, a

Edward Cowper.

very eminent professor of mechanics at one of the colleges, who had in 1818 invented several important improvements in printing appliances. Amongst these was a new method of inking, by employing a flat distributing table on which the ink was uniformly spread by rollers having a rotary motion. The ink was conveyed to the table in very small quantities at intervals by a roller which vibrated between a metal roller supplied with ink and the distributing table, to which a small quantity of ink was communicated each time that the vibrating roller touched it. Cowper took away the old inking apparatus from the "Times" machine and put in his own, and in other ways altered and simplified the machine. In 1827 he and his partner, an engineer named Augustus Applegath, constructed a new machine, for the journal; and as this was at work when the Queen ascended the throne, a short outline of its arrangements may be of interest. The forme of type was passed backwards and forwards under four cylinders; the machine being supplied with paper from four feeding boards, at each of which a boy stood to supply the sheets. Two boys stood on the floor, and two on a raised platform; four others being placed at the ends of the machine to receive the printed sheets. For the purpose of supplying the sheets to the machine the heap of paper was placed at one end of the feeding board, the boy drawing forward the top sheets by rubbing them or stroking them in with a paper knife. Each sheet was then brought in advance of that below, and the edge of the topmost sheet projected beyond the board and lodged on a wooden roller furnished with tapes which constantly revolved. The roller had no effect on the edge of the sheet until at the proper time a bar was caused to drop, and the paper, caught between two sets of tapes, was carried by them round the cylinder, where it received the impression. The tapes and sheet continued their progress until they arrived at the place where the taker-off stood, and there the tapes separated, and the sheet fell into the hands of the boy. This machine printed at the rate, then regarded as astonishing, of 4,000 per hour, on one side only. Each sheet, however, was nearly four times the size of the old newspapers printed on Koenig's machine.

This machine really comprised the mechanism of four single machines combined in one frame, all being worked simultaneously by steam as the motive power. It was in use up to 1848, when Augustus Applegath invented an apparatus on altogether new lines. This was regarded as a marvellous mechanical accomplishment; and a machine on the same principles was one of the most popular features of the Great Exhibition of 1851 in Hyde Park. In the centre of the apparatus, of which an illustration is appended, there was a cylinder about 5½ feet in diameter, which was fixed in a vertical position. The cylinders of printing machines had always previously been placed horizontally, and since this machine was superseded they have always been in the same position. The type was fastened upon the upright cylinder. Around it, as shown in the illustration, were placed eight other vertical cylinders, each about a foot in diameter. They were the paper cylinders, each of which was furnished with a feeding apparatus, whereat one boy laid on the sheets. Necessarily, this feeding apparatus was very peculiar, its

Applegath machine built for the "Times" in 1848.

object being to convey the sheet from its horizontal position on one of the feeding boards to its vertical position on the paper cylinder. Over each of the eight cylinders was a sloping desk, upon which a stock of unprinted paper was deposited. At the side of the desk stood the layer-on, who pushed the sheets towards the fingers or grippers of the machine. These grippers, seizing upon a sheet, first drew it down in a vertical direction between tapes on the eight vertical frames, until its horizontal edges corresponded with the position of the forme of type on the printing cylinder. Arrived at this position, its vertical motion was stopped by a self-acting appratus provided in the machine, and it began to move horizontally, and was thus carried towards the printing-cylinder by the tapes. As it passed round this cylinder it was impressed upon the type and printed. It was then carried back horizontally by similar tapes on the other side of the frame, until it arrived at another desk, where the taker-off awaited it. The grippers disengaging it, the taker-off received it and deposited it upon the desk. This movement went on without interruption, and the product was about 9,600 impressions per hour. Inevitable stoppages, however, arising from the number of persons participating in the working of the apparatus, very considerably reduced this nominal speed.

The next step in advance, at the office of the "Times," was the adoption in 1857 of an American press, called the "Type Revolving Printing Machine," manufactured by Col. Richard M. Hoe, of New York. This machine had been introduced into Great Britain in the previous year by the late Mr. Edward Lloyd, for the purpose of printing "Lloyd's Weekly Newspaper." It was not only more compact than the Applegath, but could be driven at a higher rate of speed. The cylinders were horizontal, there being from two to ten impression cylinders, the latter capable of giving nearly 20,000 impressions per hour, on one side of the paper only; but that rate was seldom kept up. One new feature was that the takers-off were dispensed with, by the invention of

Hoe's type revolving machine. 1857.

self-acting "flyers." These deposited the sheets upon tables
or flyboards, there being as many of these attached to the
machine as there were impression cylinders. At first movable
type was used, and it was ingeniously arranged on the larger
cylinder. Each column of type was set up on the level, but
six or seven columns, for a large newspaper, were nevertheless adjusted side by side. Brass rules of a bevelled shape, or
of wedge-like section, were placed between the columns, the
bevel varying according to the curvature of the cylinder. All
the columns of type were then adjusted and tightened up to
occupy, in polygonal fashion, a portion of the circum-
ference of the cylinder, the remaining portion affording space
for the inking rollers to act. At a later date stereotype plates,
each strictly conforming to the curvature of the cylinder,
were used on the Hoe machine, with a great increase of speed
and economy.

Up to this time single sheets of paper had alone been used.
These limited most effectively the output of the printing
machine, because one man could not feed in more than
1,000 sheets per hour—and, indeed, few men did as much.

The only means of increasing the rate of printing was by multiplying the number of impression cylinders to which the paper was fed. When these were more than six in number the complication became great, the stoppages frequent, the waste considerable, the risk of accidents serious, and the cost of the work heavy.

An entirely new era was now about to commence. In 1862, Mr. John Walter, like his predecessors, ever on the look-out

John Walter.

for improved mechanical means of production, caused experiments to be made having two objects in view—to print from a continuous roll of paper, which could be fed in automatically at any speed at which the printing cylinder could be driven, and to print both sides of the paper at once. The experiments were carried on during the six years between 1862 and 1868, and at last one machine was finished. Three more were completed by the end of 1869, when the edition of the journal

The Walter press.

was printed on them in less than half the time previously occupied, with one-fifth of the hands required for the Hoe machines, and with a much less waste of paper and other materials. Only three men were required in the actual working; one to start and stop the machine, and two to attend to the delivery of the sheets, which came out flat.

The merit of having first completed a practical rotary machine, is due to William Bullock, an engineer of Philadelphia, U.S.A., whose first press was finished in 1865, after years of patient experiment. The inventor did not long enjoy the fruits of his labours, for he was accidentally killed while testing one of his machines, in 1868. The "Daily Telegraph" had a Bullock web machine at work before the Walter press was in operation.

The next improvement which requires to be mentioned here is the invention of the "Supplement" press, manufactured by Messrs. Hoe and Co., of New York and London. It prints a journal of variable sizes, of 8, 10, 12, 16, 20, or 24 pages; it cuts the sheets, fits them together, and folds them, and finally delivers them on the receiver counted into quires of 27 copies, or any number that may be desired. The illustration shows a cartload of reels of paper on the road to the printing office. This has now become quite an ordinary sight in London, and is passed by in the street without remark.

Delivery of paper in reels.

It is a great contrast to the old plan of delivering the paper in reams; and, simple though it seems, marks the climax of a long series of mechanical successes in the paper mill, as well as in the printing office.

When the paper is delivered it is quite dry, and as it receives the ink from the plates in the printing process best when it is somewhat damp, it has to be passed through a wetting machine. The reel, as it goes through this machine, is pressed against an iron cylinder, which dips into a trough of water, and thus the paper is damped. In the engraving one reel of

Reel damping machine.

paper is nearly finished wetting. The man is standing against
the wetted reel, which is growing bigger and bigger as the dry
reel at the rear end of the machine is growing smaller and
smaller. The reel, which may be about six feet wide and four
miles in length, has to be lifted on to and off the machine
by means of a crane, as it is far too heavy to move anyhow
else, weighing nearly three-quarters of a ton.

The Hoe Double Supplement Press is capable of printing,
cutting, and folding 24,000 copies per hour of a full-sized
newspaper of eight, ten, or more pages. The main reel is
shown on the left hand of the illustration; it is 75 inches
wide and 36 inches in diameter. The supplement reel, 37½
inches wide, is on the right hand. The plates on the main part
of the press are not visible in the drawing, but those for the
supplement portion are shown, in cylindrical form, parallel
to the spindle of the supplement reel, but on the level of the
head of the attendant. The stereo plates are first attached to
two large cylinders, and if there is an enlarged paper the plates
for these are put on the supplement portion. The chief reel
of paper is suspended close to the floor and fed into the
machine between the face of the stereotype plates and the

Hoe supplement press, present day.

impression cylinder covered with blanket. The first cylinder prints it on one side, and it is conveyed to the next, which prints it on the other. The ink fountain is placed over the large cylinder, and is surrounded by rollers of varying size up to six inches in diameter, which distribute it on to the inking rollers. The cylinders bearing the plates revolve 200 times every minute. The paper is printed before it is cut up. It is passed upwards and over rollers at the top of the machine, and as it goes, a revolving knife presses upon it at right angles with the width and divides it into two longitudinal lengths. These two sheets then pass over bars, which turn them at right angles to their original direction, and they immediately meet the supplement sheet coming from its own part of the machine, which passes in between the two main sheets. Supplement and twin lengths are carried together over and down the outer surface of the sloping triangular steel plate, or "former," with the apex at the bottom. The sheets curl over and under the edges of the "former," until they are drawn together in the proper order of their numbered pages between a pair of horizontal rollers. Still the length of these sheets remains connected with the web as it unrolls. Now, however, the whole set of pages encounter cylinders armed with knives with a saw-like edge, sheathed in indiarubber beds, which separate the connection, while the folding blade of a cylinder opposite creases down the middle between the pages. The latter then pass through small rollers that fold over the papers on the line of the crease, and the newspaper is finished. A rotary fly deposits the papers on to a set of leather bands, which are continuously travelling forward, and on which the papers rapidly accumulate—a gap between every 27 copies denoting a quire. The engraving shows the method of clearing away the folded papers from the delivery part of the machine.

There are several other kinds of supplement machines made by various makers. Amongst these may be mentioned the Victory machine on which many newspapers of large

Clearing the delivery.

circulation are printed. It was the inventor of this machine, the late Mr. G. A. Wilson, who, in 1870, first added a folding apparatus, which turned out the copies ready for sale by the newsagents. A first-class web machine of the present day will print and fold four and six-page papers at the rate of 48,000 copies per hour; eight, ten, and twelve-page papers at the rate of 24,000 copies per hour; and sixteen, twenty, or twenty-four-page papers at the rate of 12,000 per hour—all cut at the head, and counted in bundles of any number required. Such machines are arranged for three independent rolls of paper, each roll having its own complete printing mechanism. One of the most popular weeklies is printed at the highest rate of speed on a machine of this kind, which, besides folding the paper into quarto pages, puts on the wrappers, and wire-stitches them.

Bookwook, including periodical work, was done, in the year 1837 on Applegath and Cowper's Perfecting Machine, the general features of which have already been indicated.

The Applegath and
Cowper machine.

There were then, however, very few offices indeed which required such a costly apparatus. This style of printing was almost entirely restricted to the hand press, mainly for two reasons. When editions were small it was cheapest to print them at press. There was, too, in existence a general prejudice against machine work. It was thought that fine printing could not be obtained by the employment of the cylinder principle, and that the platen was the only expedient that would give satisfactory results. In view of the many imperfections of the machines of sixty years ago, this objection to them was to a certain extent well founded. It has now entirely disappeared. The very finest "art" work is produced on cylinder machines, and with a cleanness of impression, solidity, and brilliancy, accuracy of register, and uniformity of colour that no hand press could possibly accomplish. Certain classes of printing, such as that of process blocks, could not be done at all on a press, because the requisite strength of impression could not possibly be obtained from it. Jobbing printing, too, is now almost invariably produced by machine. There are two kinds of machines for doing this kind of work. One is a cylinder machine, in which the type forme is placed on a flat bed, on a carriage which travels backward and forward. At one point in its journey it receives the ink from composition rollers, and at another it is brought, with the paper on the top of it, under the pressure of the cylinder. There are elaborate mechanical arrangements for ensuring a regulated supply of ink to the rollers, and giving a firm unshrinking pressure on the types. The other class of machine is known as the small platen machine. The platen and the type forme are in a vertical position perfectly parallel to each other at the time of impression. The paper being fed in between them, they are brought gradually together, and their degree of proximity is so regulated that the platen gives a quick but perfectly solid impact upon the forme. The attendant simply lays on and takes off the sheet; all the rest is done automatically. Some presses of this kind have a mechanical delivery, so that feeding them is all that is necessary.

* * * * *

Process Blocks—Line Blocks—Tone Blocks—Method of Their Production.

There are two kinds of process blocks, known as "line blocks" and "tone blocks." The first, of which the "Photo Printing Room" block is a specimen, are made from drawings in pen and ink, and from printed engravings in line and stipple. The drawing is first taken into the photographic studio, in which cameras of unusually large size—some of them capable of producing a negative measuring 24 by 24 inches—are mounted on sliding platforms, as shown in the illustration. In the City of London the electric light is found to be the best illuminant, as the almost invariably murky atmosphere scarcely ever affords sufficient light for the purpose even on the brightest of days. Photographing by electric light can be carried on during the night-time, which is of importance when great despatch in the production of blocks is required. The plate glass for the negative is prepared in the customary manner of the collodion process, and after exposure in the camera the plate goes to the dark room, where it is developed. It is afterwards intensified and fixed. After this it goes to the printing room, the arrangements of which may be as shown

Photographic studio for reproduction for process blocks.

in the illustration. This stage of the process is one of the most important features of the art of photo-etching, as much of the ultimate success depends upon the proper preparation of the zinc plate upon which the picture is transferred from the negative. All blemishes, such as spots and scratches, have to be carefully obliterated, and the surface must be highly polished, without having an extreme smoothness. For this reason the plate is immersed in a weak acid bath, which gives it a grained character. A sensitising solution is then poured over the plate, which is next dried over gas. It is next placed on the negative in a printing frame in the manner adopted by photographers generally. The negative is placed on the glass, and the sensitised zinc pressed firmly and evenly upon it by boards and screws. The glazed front is exposed to the powerful rays of the electric light for a period regulated by the power of the illuminant and the density wished for in the

Photo printing-room for process work.

negative. This is ascertained by the use of the actinometer. When sufficiently exposed the plate is removed from the frame, rolled up with lithographic transfer ink, and developed in a bath containing water. By gently rubbing with cotton wool the sensitised film is removed, except in those places where the light has acted upon it through the picture. The parts so fixed are the actual lines of the original picture, which now appears black on a light ground. The plate is dried, the entire surface covered with gum arabic, dried again, and again rolled up with ink. All this gives the lines of the drawing a firm acid "resist," the ink being fixed to the plate by means of a coating of resin. What is called "retouching" may, however, be necessary at this stage in order to rectify the defects of the original from which the photograph was taken. When dry, the plate is taken to a litho press, and an impression on transfer paper from a copper-plate having

Etching-room for process work.

the required tint engraved upon it is placed upon the zinc plate, and the whole run through the litho press. It will then be found that, except where the surface has been gummed, the lines or dots have been transferred to the spaces originally assigned to them by the artist. The plate next goes to the etching-room, of which an illustration is appended. Here the large surfaces which will appear white when printed, are painted out by a solution of shellac, which resists acid, and when this is dry the plate is given a first bath of very much diluted nitric acid. This mixture is contained in a very large earthenware pan or trough. One effect of the action of the acid upon the metal is the formation of oxides and air bubbles, which have to be got rid of, either by gently swaying the trough, which is balanced on rockers, so as to keep the acid in motion, or by a system of brushing the plates while in the bath with a camel-hair brush. Every plate must go though various stages of etching in baths of various strengths, but between each bath the more delicate parts of the design are painted out, and the plate rolled up. At length there remain only the large spaces, which must be eaten away to a considerable depth by the nitric acid. The plate is cleaned, and a proof is pulled on the press in order to judge the result. If defects are observable they may be rectified by an engraver. The plate is finally mounted on a wood block, generally of oak, to make it type-high.

For reproducing photographs, drawings in wash, pencil, and chalk, and all kinds of paintings and drawings in colour, the "half-tone" process is employed. The expression "half-tone" is a translation into English of the familiar art phrase, "mezzo-tinto." The distinctive feature of a process block of this kind is that the various tones in the original are reproduced, not by lines, but by minute dots. The illustration, "Photographic Studio," is an example of this style of process block. The dots are not always detected by the unassisted eye, but they can be readily perceived by the use of a magnifying glass. This texture is produced by means of a screen placed in the camera between the lens and the negative. The screen may be formed by two sheets of glass attached to each other, each having upon its inner surface a series of minutely-engraved parallel lines. On one plate these lines are vertical, and on the other horizontal, or they may be engraved diagonally, to the right and left respectively. The engraved lines cut up into minute squares the image of the picture as it appears in the negative. The subsequent processes for making the tone block are substantially the same as for the line block. In order to "bite in" the plate it is passed through weak acid and rolled up with ink. It is then laid in a stone trough containing an acid solution to be "deep etched"—that is, until the acid has eaten away all that is necessary of the darkest portion of the picture. Every plate goes through several baths, between each of which it is dusted with an acid-resisting powder, and proofs are taken during the progress of the work.

The introduction of the half-tone block has almost revolutionised modern methods of printing. The old conditions of using damp paper and a blanketed cylinder have had to be abandoned, and a special paper produced to suit the new kind of illustration. A wood-cut is almost as easily printed as a type forme, on account of the high relief of the surface, but the tone process block is so slightly in relief that its depth is not appreciable to the touch. To obtain a fine impression super-calendered paper has to be used, in which all the microscopic interstices have been levelled up by filling them with a calcareous deposit, and finishing by heavy rolling. The printing machine has had to be re-modelled by making it three times as strong to bear the strain of the rigidity of the cylinder when in contact with the hard copper blocks.

William Morris

A Note by William Morris on his aims in founding the Kelmscott Press

1898.

I began printing books with the hope of producing some which would have a definite claim to beauty, while at the same time they should be easy to read and should not dazzle the eye, or trouble the intellect of the reader by eccentricity of form in the letters. I have always been a great admirer of the calligraphy of the Middle Ages, and of the earlier printing which took its place. As to the fifteenth century books, I had noticed that they were always beautiful by force of the mere typography, even without the added ornament, with which many of them are so lavishly supplied. And it was the essence of my undertaking to produce books which it would be a pleasure to look upon as pieces of printing and arrangement of type. Looking at my adventure from this point of view then, I found I had to consider chiefly the following things: the paper, the form of the type, the relative spacing of the letters, the words, and the lines, and lastly the position of the printed matter on the page.

It was a matter of course that I should consider it necessary that the paper should be hand-made, both for the sake of durability and appearance. It would be a very false economy to stint in the quality of the paper as to price: so I had only to think about the kind of hand-made paper. On this head I came to two conclusions: 1st, that the paper must be wholly of linen (most hand-made papers are of cotton to-day), and must be quite "hard," i.e. thoroughly well sized; and 2nd, that though it must be "laid" and not "wove" (i.e. made on a mould made of obvious wires), the lines caused by the wires of the mould must not be too strong, so as to give a ribbed appearance. I found that on these points I was at one with the practice of the papermakers of the fifteenth century; so I took as my model a Bolognese paper of about 1473. My friend Mr. Batchelor, of Little Chart, Kent, carried out my views very satisfactorily, and produced from the first the excellent paper which I still use.

Next as to type. By instinct rather than by conscious thinking it over, I began by getting myself a fount of Roman type. And here what I wanted was letter pure in form; severe, without needless excrescences; solid, without the thickening and thinning of the line, which is the essential fault of the ordinary modern type, and which makes it difficult to read; and not compressed laterally, as all later type has grown to be owing to commercial exigencies. There was only one source from which to take examples of this perfected Roman type, to wit, the works of the great Venetian printers of the fifteenth century, of whom Nicholas Jenson produced the completest and most Roman characters from 1470 to 1476. This type I studied with much care, getting it photographed to a big scale, and drawing it over many times before I began

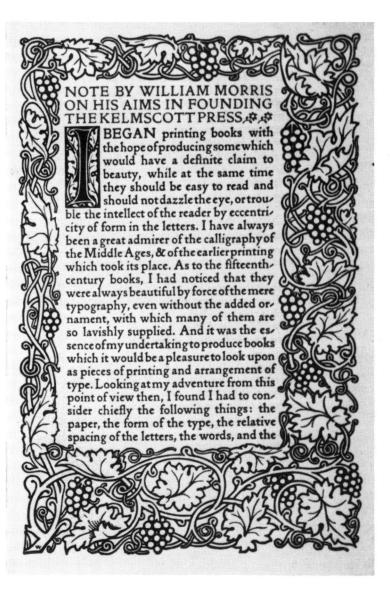

NOTE BY WILLIAM MORRIS
ON HIS AIMS IN FOUNDING
THE KELMSCOTT PRESS.✿ ✿

I BEGAN printing books with the hope of producing some which would have a definite claim to beauty, while at the same time they should be easy to read and should not dazzle the eye, or trouble the intellect of the reader by eccentricity of form in the letters. I have always been a great admirer of the calligraphy of the Middle Ages, & of the earlier printing which took its place. As to the fifteenth-century books, I had noticed that they were always beautiful by force of the mere typography, even without the added ornament, with which many of them are so lavishly supplied. And it was the essence of my undertaking to produce books which it would be a pleasure to look upon as pieces of printing and arrangement of type. Looking at my adventure from this point of view then, I found I had to consider chiefly the following things: the paper, the form of the type, the relative spacing of the letters, the words, and the designing my own letter; so that though I think I mastered the essence of it, I did not copy it servilely; in fact, my Roman type, especially in the lower case, tends rather more to the Gothic than does Jenson's.

After a while I felt that I must have a Gothic as well as a Roman fount; and herein the task I set myself was to redeem the Gothic character from the charge of unreadableness which is commonly brought against it. And I felt that this charge could not be reasonably brought against the types of the first two decades of printing: that Schoeffer at Mainz, Mentelin at Strasburg, and Gunther Zainer at Augsburg, avoided the spiky ends and undue compression which lay some of the later printers open to the above charge. Only the earlier printers (naturally following therein the practice of their predecessors the scribes) were very liberal of contractions, and used an excess of "tied" letters, which, by the way, are very useful to the compositor. So I entirely eschewed contractions, except for the "&," and had very few tied letters, in fact none but the absolutely necessary ones. Keeping my end steadily in view, I designed a black-letter type which I think I may claim to be as readable as a Roman one, and to say the truth I prefer it to the Roman. This type is of the size called Great Primer (the Roman type is of "English" size); but later on I was driven by the necessities of the Chaucer (a double-columned book) to get a smaller Gothic type of Pica size.

The punches for all these types, I may mention, were cut for me with great intelligence and skill by Mr. E. P. Prince, and render my designs most satisfactorily.

Now as to the spacing. First, the "face" of the letter should be as nearly conterminous with the "body" as possible, so as to avoid undue whites between the letters. Next, the lateral spaces between the words should be (a) no more than is necessary to distinguish clearly the division into words, and (b) should be as nearly equal as possible. Modern printers, even the best, pay very little heed to these two essentials of seemly composition, and the inferior ones run riot in licentious spacing, thereby producing, *inter alia*, those ugly rivers of lines running about the page which are such a blemish to decent printing. Third, the whites between the lines should not be excessive; the modern practice of "leading" should be used as little as possible, and never without some definite reason, such as marking some special piece of printing. The only leading I have allowed myself is in some cases a "thin" lead between the lines of my Gothic pica type; in the Chaucer and the double-columned books I have used a "hair" lead, and not even this in the 16mo books. Lastly, but by no means least, comes the position of the printed matter on the page. This should always leave the inner margin the narrowest, the top somewhat wider, the outside (fore-edge) wider still, and the bottom widest of all. This rule is never departed from in medieval books, written or printed. Modern printers systematically transgress against it; thus apparently contradicting the fact that the unit of a book is not one page, but a pair of pages. A friend, the librarian of one of our most important private libraries, tells me that after careful testing he has come to the conclusion that the medieval rule was to make a difference of 20 per cent from margin to margin. Now these matters of spacing and position are of the greatest importance in the production of beautiful books; if they are properly considered they will make a book printed in quite ordinary type at least decent and pleasant to the eye. The disregard of them will spoil the effect of the best designed type.

It was only natural that I, a decorator by profession, should attempt to ornament my books suitably; about this matter I will only say that I have always tried to keep in mind the necessity for making my decoration a part of the page of type. I may add that in designing the magnificent and inimitable woodcuts that have adorned several of my books, and will above all adorn the Chaucer which is now drawing near to completion, my friend Sir Edward Burne-Jones has never lost sight of this important point, so that his work will not only give us a series of most beautiful and imaginative pictures, but form the most harmonious decoration possible to the printed book.

KELMSCOTT HOUSE,
UPPER MALL, HAMMERSMITH,
Nov. 11, 1895.

Eric Gill

An Essay on Typography
(1931). 1954. pp. 46-51, 68-69

The business of poster letters has not yet been extricated from the degradations imposed upon it by an insubordinate commercialism. Mere weight and heaviness of letter ceases to be effective in assisting the comprehension of the reader when every poster plays the same shouting game. A man at whom twenty brick-manufacturers throw bricks from every side at once is quite unable to distinguish the qualities in which 'Blue Staffordshires' are superior to 'London Stocks'. A return to mere legibility seems desirable even if the effect be less striking. To this end it is necessary to study the principles of legibility—the characters which distinguish one letter from another, the proportions of light and dark in letters and spacing.

A square or oblong with its corners rounded off may, by itself, be more like an O than anything else, but in conjunction with a D made on the same principles there is not much by which to recognise which is which, and from a distance the two are indistinguishable. Many engineers affect this style of letter, believing it to be devoid of that 'art-nonsense' on the absence of which they pride themselves.

1 & 2 show the engineers' O & D, hardly distinguish-
able from one another; 3 & 4 show forms equally
black, no wider, but more legible, which are suitable
where the space required for the normal, 5 & 6, is not
available.

That newspaper-vendors should use the same style of letter is
even more surprising. If the aims of engineers and newsagents were purely decorative, we could more easily appreciate their efforts, even though, to our more rational minds,
names on locomotives and advertisements of the contents of
more or less untrustworthy journals seem alike unnecessary.

Legibility, in practice, amounts simply to what one is
accustomed to. But this is not to say that because we have
got used to something demonstrably less legible than something else would be if we could get used to it, we should
make no effort to scrap the existing thing. This was done by
the Florentines and Romans of the fifteenth century; it
requires simply good sense in the originators & good will
in the rest of us.

Good will seems to be the common possession of mankind,
but its complement, good sense, i.e. intelligence, critical
ability, and that intense concentration upon precise perfection which is a kind of genius, is not so common. Good will

comes from below & occasionally penetrates into studios and cabinets. Good sense comes from above & percolates thro' the mass of people. Everybody thinks that he knows an A when he sees it; but only the few extraordinary rational minds can distinguish between a good one & a bad one, or can demonstrate precisely what constitutes A-ness. When is an A not an A? Or when is an R not an R? It is clear that for any letter there is some sort of norm. To discover this norm is obviously the first thing to be done.

The first notable attempt to work out the norm for plain letters was made by Mr Edward Johnston when he designed the sans-serif letter for the London Underground Railways. Some of these letters are not entirely satisfactory, especially when it is remembered that, for such a purpose, an alphabet should be as near as possible 'fool-proof', i.e. the forms should be measurable, patient of dialectical exposition, as the philosophers would say—nothing should be left to the imagination of the sign-writer or the enamel-plate maker. In this quality of 'fool-proofness' the Monotype sans-serif face is perhaps an improvement. The letters are more strictly normal—freer from forms depending upon appreciation and critical ability in the workman who has to reproduce them.

ABCDEFGHIJKLM
NOPQRSTUVWX
Y&Z 1234567890
abcdefghijklmno
pqrstuvwxyz

Monotype sans-serif.

But, as there is a norm of letter form—the bare body, so to say, of letters—there is also a norm of letter clothes: or rather there are many norms according as letters are used for this place or purpose or that. Between the occasion wherein the pure sans-serif or mono-line (block) letter is appropriate & that in which nothing is more appropriate than pure fancifulness there are innumerable occasions.

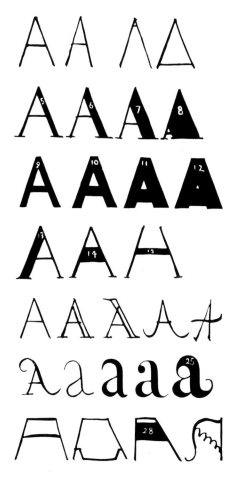

Essential form; 2, too narrow; 3 & 4, absurd misconceptions; 5 & 6, normal; 7, overbold; 8, suitable for advertisements of 'Bovril'; 9, normal sans-serif; 10, sans bold; 11, sans overbold; 12, hardly recognisable; 13 & 14, thick and thin unusually disposed; 15, A undecided as to whether it is an A or an aitch; 16 & 17, normal; 18, top-heavy; 19, a decent variation; 20, a poor thing but might be worse; 21, a fancy possibility; 22, essential form of lower-case a; 23, normal type form; 24, Victorian vulgarity; 25, comic variety; 26-29, A's that are not A's.

Typography (the reproduction of lettering by means of movable letter types) was originally done by pressing the inked surface or 'face' of a letter made of wood or metal against a surface of paper or vellum. The unevenness and hardness of paper, the irregularities of types (both in respect of their printing faces and the dimensions of their 'bodies') and the mechanical imperfections of presses and printing methods made the work of early printers notable for corresponding unevenesses, irregularities & mechanical imperfections. To ensure that every letter left its mark more or less completely & evenly, considerable and noticeable impression was made in the paper. The printed letter was a coloured letter at the bottom of a ditch.

The subsequent development of typography was chiefly the development of technical improvements, more accurately cast types, smoother paper, mechanically perfect presses. Apart from the history of its commercial exploitation, the history of printing has been the history of the abolition of the impression. A print is properly a dent made by pressing; the history of letterpress printing has been the history of the abolition of that dent.

But the very smooth paper and the mechanically very perfect presses required for printing which shall show no 'impression' can only be produced in a world which cares for such things, and such a world is of its nature inhuman. The industrial world of to-day is such, and it has the printing it desires and deserves. In the industrial world Typography, like house-building & sanitary engineering, is one of the necessary arts—a thing to be done in working hours, those during which one is buoyed up by the knowledge that one is serving one's fellow men, and neither enjoying oneself like an artist nor praising God like a man of prudence. In such a world the only excuse for anything is that it is of service. Printing which makes any claim on its own account, printers who give themselves the status of poets or painters, are to be condemned; they are not serving; they are shirking. Such is the tone of the more romantic among men of commerce; and the consequence is a pseudo-asceticism & a bastard aesthetic. The asceticism is only a sham because the test of service is the profits shown in the accounts; and the aesthetic is bastard because it is not founded upon the reasonable pleasure of the mind of the workman and of his customer, but upon the snobbery of museum students employed by men of commerce to give a saleable appearance to articles too dull otherwise to please even the readers of the Daily Mail.

Stanley Morison

First Principles of Typography

(1930). 1951. pp. 5-8

I Novelty in printing

Letters of the alphabet that are case or founded for the purpose of impressing upon paper are known as 'types' and the impression thus made as a 'print'. But every impression, from any raised surface, is a 'print'. Hence the impression from the particular raised surfaces known as 'types' is called a 'typographical' impression; or, to use a more old-fashioned term, 'letter-press'. The precise form of the 'types' and the exact position they need to occupy upon the selected paper involve skill in the art that is called 'typography'.

Typography may be defined as the art of rightly disposing printing material in accordance with specific purpose; of so arranging the letters, distributing the space and controlling the type as to aid to the maximum the reader's comprehension of the text. Typography is the efficient means to an essentially utilitarian and only accidentally aesthetic end, for enjoyment of patterns is rarely the reader's chief aim. Therefore, any disposition of printing material which, whatever the intention, has the effect of coming between author and reader is wrong. It follows that in the printing of books meant to be read there is little room for 'bright' typography. Even dullness and monotony in the typesetting are far less vicious to a reader than typographical eccentricity or pleasantry. Cunning of this sort is desirable, even essential in the typography of propaganda, whether for commerce, politics, or religion, because in such printing only the freshest survives inattention. But the typography of books, apart from the category of narrowly limited editions, requires an obedience to convention which is almost absolute—and with reason.

Since printing is essentially a means of multiplying, it must not only be good in itself—but be good for a common purpose. The wider that purpose, the stricter are the limitations imposed upon the printer. He may try an experiment in a tract printed in an edition of 50 copies, but he shows little common sense if he experiments to the same degree in the tract having a run of 50,000. Again, a novelty, fitly introduced into a 16-page pamphlet, will be highly undesirable in a 160-page book. It is of the essence of typography and of the nature of the printed book *qua* book, that it perform a public service. For single or individual purpose there remains the manuscript, the codex; so there is something ridiculous in the unique copy of a printed book, though the number of copies printed may justifiably be limited when a book is the medium of typographical experiment. It is always desirable that experiments be made, and it is a pity that such 'laboratory' pieces are so limited in number and in courage. Typography to-day does not so much need Inspiration or Revival as Investigation. It is proposed here to formulate some of the principles already known to book-printers, which investigation confirms and which non-printers may like to consider for themselves.

II Design of type

The laws governing the typography of books intended for general circulation are based first upon the essential nature of alphabetical writing, and secondly upon the traditions, explicit or implicit, prevailing in the society for which the printer is working. While a universal character or typography applicable to all books produced in a given national area is practicable, to impose a universal detailed formula upon all books printed in roman types is not. National tradition expresses itself in the varying separation of the book into prelims, chapters, etc., no less than in the design of the type. But at least there are physical rules of linear composition which are obeyed by all printers who know their job.

The normal roman type (in simple form without special sorts, etc.) consists of an upright design, and a sloping form of it:

– ABCDEFGHIJKLMNOPQRSTUVWXYZ&
– ABCDEFGHIJKLMNOPQRSTUVWXYZ
– abcdefghijklmnopqrstuvwxyz
– *ABCDEFGHIJKLMNOPQRSTUVWXYZ&*
– *abcdefghijklmnopqrstuvwxyz*

The printer needs to be very careful in choosing his type, realizing that the more often he is going to use it, the more closely its design must approximate to the general idea held in the mind's eye of readers perforce ruled by the familiar magazine, newspaper and book. It does no harm to print a Christmas card in 𝔟𝔩𝔞𝔠𝔨 𝔩𝔢𝔱𝔱𝔢𝔯, but who nowadays would read a book in that type? I may believe, as I do, that black letter is in design more homogeneous, more lively and more economic a type than the grey round roman we use, but I do not now expect people to read a book in it. Aldus' and Caslon's are both relatively feeble types, but they represent the forms accepted by the community; and the printer, as a servant of the community, must use them, or one of their variants. No printer should say, 'I am an artist, therefore I am not to be dictated to. I will create my own letter forms', for, in this humble job, no printer is an artist in this sense. Nor is it possible to-day, as it just was in the infancy of the craft, to persuade society into the acceptance of strongly marked and highly individualistic types—because literate society is so much greater in mass and correspondingly slower in movement. Type design moves at the pace of the most conservative reader. The good type-designer therefore realizes that, for a new fount to be successful, it has to be so good that only very few recognize its novelty. If readers do not notice the consummate reticence and rare discipline of a new type, it is probably a good letter. But if my friends think that the tail of my lower-case r or the lip of my lower-case e is rather jolly, you may know that the fount would have been better had neither been made. A type which is to have anything like a present, let alone a future, will neither be very 'different' nor very 'jolly'.

Jan Tschichold

Die neue Typographie

1928. pp. 65-68, translated by C. Ashwin

THE PRINCIPLES OF THE NEW TYPOGRAPHY

Every day contemporary man has to assimilate an enormous amount of printed material, whether he has ordered it or not, which is delivered to his home or which he encounters out of doors in posters, shop windows, directional signs etc. In respect of the production of printed material, the modern age differs from the past primarily not so much through form as through quantity. However, with the increase in quantity the form of printed material will also be subject to changes: for the speed with which today's consumer of printed matter must be able to absorb what is printed, the lack of time, which forces him to use the maximum economy in the reading process, inevitably demands also an adaptation of the 'form' to the circumstances of contemporary life. As a rule we no longer read in a leisurely way line for line, but attempt at first to scan the whole, and only when our interest is awakened to study the material more thoroughly.

The old style of typography, in regard to its mental content as well as its form, is adapted to earlier generations of man, who, not oppressed by lack of time, could peacefully read line by line. In those days, functionalism had no meaningful role to play. Hence the old typography concerned itself less with function than with something which one described as 'beauty', 'art', or something similar. Problems of formal aesthetics (the choice of letter form, combination of letter forms, use of ornament) occupied the foreground of interest. Consequently the history of typography since Manutius is not so much a development to greater clarity and purity of appearance (the only exceptions are the periods of Didot, Bodoni, Baskerville and Walbaum), but as a phenomenon concurrent with the development of historical letterform and ornament.

It was reserved for our own time to achieve a living place for the problem of 'form'. While one previously regarded the form as something external, as a product of 'artistic invention' (Haeckel even endowed nature with such 'artistic intentions' in his 'Art forms in nature'), these days by means of a renewed study of nature, and above all of technology (which is only a secondary form of nature), we have come considerably closer to a real understanding of its true character. Nature and technology both teach us that 'form' is not something independent, but grows out of function (the purpose, specification), the nature of materials used (organic or technological materials), and the organic, that is to say, technical, construction. This is how the wonderful forms of nature, and the no less wonderful forms of technology, have originated. One may define the forms of technology as equally 'organic' (in the spiritual sense), as those of nature. But even the forms of technology are regarded by many as something external, and they marvel at the 'beauty' of an aircraft, an automobile, a steamship, instead of recognising that their completed appearance is nothing other than the precise, economical expression of their function. In the process of the creation of forms, technology and nature follow the same laws of economy, precision, minimum friction, etc; whereas, however, technology should never take its specification from a self-fulfilling purpose, but should only serve as a means, and thus impinges only indirectly on the mental life of man, the other areas of human form-making elevate themselves because of their spiritual nature above the purely functional character of merely technological forms. But even these, in response to natural laws, aspire to ever-greater clarity and purity of appearance. So architecture liberates itself from facade ornament and 'ornamental' furniture and develops its forms out of the functions of the building—no longer from the outside to the inside, as the facade mentality of the period before the war prescribed, but from the inside to the outside, which is the natural way. In the same fashion, typography, too, freed itself from the preceding, formalistic-external appearance, from the merely superficial 'traditional' long deal schemes. We perceive in the succession of historical styles, such as the reaction which came after the Jugendstil, nothing more than an evidence of creative incapacity. It can no longer be accepted these days, to desire to aspire to the dated typographical master works of earlier centuries by simply apeing them. Our time, with its quite different tasks, the often essentially changed means, and with its highly developed technology, necessitates new, quite different forms of appearance. Today, even to see in the Gutenberg Bible, whose great historical significance is undisputed, a 'never-more-attainable' ideal, is naive, unfounded romanticism, which it is high time we abandoned. If we wish to 'prove ourselves worthy' of the significant achievements of earlier times, then we must set them against the achievements of our own born out of our own time. They can only then become 'classic', when they are unhistorical.

The essence of the new typography is clarity. This places it in conscious opposition to the old typography, which proceeds from a conception of 'beauty' and which does not satisfy today's exceptional demand for clarity. This extreme clarity is necessary because the multifarious demands placed upon contemporary man by the extraordinary quantity of printed matter requires the maximum economy of expression. The gentle alternation between ornamental scripts, of externally perceived 'beautiful' letter forms, and decoration by means of alien trimmings (ornament) can never produce the pure form such as we demand.

Above all the feeble adherence to the bugbear of centralised design has created the greatest sterility in previous typography.

In the old typography, the external arrangement of individual groups is subjected to the principle of centring. In the introductory historical section I have stated that this principle appeared with the renaissance and has never since been abandoned. The purely external nature of this formal principle is evident in typical renaissance and baroque title pages.

There, the main ideas are quite arbitrarily cut up; logical sequence, which should for example express itself in the use of different sizes of type, is sacrificed regardless to external form, so that the main line shows only three-quarters of the main idea, the rest being taken up several sizes smaller in the next group of type. Admittedly, this sort of thing is quite rare these days, but the inflexibility of axial design still prevents a reform according to a logical point of view to the degree required by modern life. As an invisible artificial spine, centred design runs through the whole and creates a false sense of inner unity, rather like the Wilhelmine five-centimetre high stiff collar. Even in good centred composition, content is sacrificed to 'beautiful line sequence'; the whole is a 'form' which is predetermined, and therefore must be inorganic.

In my view it is mistaken to compose a test as if the middle of the lines were some kind of point of special emphasis which would justify this arrangement. This is simply not the case, for the words are read from one side to the other (we Europeans, for example, read from left to right and downwards, the Chinese from the top to the bottom, and from right to left). The fact that the distance of the stressed points from the beginning and the end of the word sequence are not the same, but quite different (and in ever-changing relationship), in itself proves the logical incorrectness of axial design. However, it is not only the rigidly prescribed formal principle of axial composition, but everything else about it—such as the pseudo-constructivism—which is opposed to the nature of the new typography. Every typographic tradition, no matter of what kind, which proceeds from a prescribed formal idea is false. **The new typography distinguishes itself from the old by virtue of the fact that it takes as its foremost objective to develop the appearance from the function of the text. The content of the printed matter must be given pure and direct expression.** Its 'form' must, as in the works of technology and those of nature, be fashioned from its function. It is only in this way that we will achieve a new typography which corresponds to the stage of mental development of modern man. The functions of a text are the objectives of communication, emphasis (word value) and the logical flow of content. **Every part of a text stands in a certain relation to every other in regard to a specific, logical pattern of emphasis and word-value, and this relation is prescribed. It is therefore up to the typographer to give the text an unambiguous visible expression, through relationships of size and weight, line sequence, colour, photography, etc.**

Harold Ernest Burtt

The Psychology of Advertising

1938. pp. 286-291

Unity

Structure.   One technique for keeping the attention adjusted upon an advertisement for an adequate length of time is to give the layout a certain inherent unity. If the different parts are related so that the reader's attention may shift from one to another easily, he may remain adjusted to the advertisement in making these shifts rather than transferring his attention elsewhere. This unity may be achieved by a structure in which all the parts form a general design. This principle is especially effective when a number of faces appear in the advertisement, all looking in the same direction. In everyday life, imitation causes one to notice where another person has his eyes directed and to look in that same direction. This tendency operates when the person to be imitated is merely a picture of a man looking at the product. If several people in the advertisement are doing likewise the effect is enhanced.

The same principle makes it inadvisable to portray a person looking away from the center of the advertisement toward an adjacent advertisement or the next page. Such an arrangement leads the reader away from the product on which it is desired to keep his attention.

Pointers. Another method of directing attention is by means of printed features which actually point in a certain direction. Just as we follow a person's gaze, so we follow his finger if he points, and in less personal fashion we are directed by an arrow or other device that has a directional aspect. If the reader's eye movements can be forced in the desired direction, his attention may be controlled, for eye movement is an important part of the total adjustment involved in an act of attention. An arrowhead or a line with a sharp member at the end directs attention in mechanical fashion, but still with some degree of effectiveness. In other instances a picture of the commodity itself is utilized in the process of pointing. If the product consists of pens or pencils, a pattern may be arranged with a number of them on the radii of a circle, all pointing toward the center where the trade name or some important selling point is presented. A violation of the above principle occurs in the advertisement for rifle cartridges which displays them all in the horizontal position, pointing out of the advertisement altogether. Sometimes instead of actual arrows or pointed objects a series of lines may connect important parts of the advertisement and hold them together. An advertisement for spark plugs showed a large picture of the plug at one side and straight lines leading from this to several small cuts of automobiles, airplanes, motor cycles, and stationary engines in which spark plugs were used. The interconnecting lines gave the layout an inherent unity.

Borders may be employed to keep attention in the advertisement. The supposition that once the attention has been directed inside the advertisement it will be difficult for the reader to surmount the border is based on the demonstrable resistance involved when the eye has to jump over a line. The principle may be demonstrated by presenting two straight lines of the same length, one of them plain and the other with short cross-lines extending its entire length. An uninformed subject will report that the latter line is longer than the former. As the eye sweeps along the line and meets these frequent obstructions, a little effort is involved in jumping over them. This greater muscular effort is erroneously interpreted as greater distance, and consequently the length of the line is over-estimated. In the same way the border of the advertisement may offer an obstruction, and the reader may not make the effort necessary to transcend it. The border is more valuable for a small advertisement than for a full page. The latter is not competing so markedly with adjacent displays. Even so, the full-page advertisements in an earlier era used borders extensively. In 1900 about 80 per cent of the full-page advertisements in some media carried borders, but at the present time the percentage is less than 30. A few concerns still maintain a small conventional border on their full-page advertisements. There is no reason to suspect that such a border does any harm providing it is not too heavy or ornate, so that it actually takes attention away from the rest of the advertisement. For certain products it may even contribute a little artistic atmosphere appropriate to the commodity.

Feelings and Attention

The methods discussed can be used to control the fluctuations of attention by mechanical factors in the construction of the advertisement. Another method for prolonging this adjustment of the organism for favorable reception of the advertisement involves the arousal of pleasant feelings. It is a familiar fact in everyday life that one tends to prolong a pleasant experience and to avoid an unpleasant one. The principle may be demonstrated experimentally. A subject in the laboratory makes movements with his forearm pivoted at the elbow and attempts to reproduce a designated angular distance with his eyes closed. If numerous readings are taken when he is in a pleasant attitude it will be observed that he moves the arm through a greater angle than is correct, whereas the reverse tendency is found if his attitude is unpleasant. The former condition involves increased use of the extensor muscles which are normally employed in reaching out toward a desired object. Similarly, in an experiment in which the subject grasps a dynamometer to record the strength of his grip, the pleasant or unpleasant character of attendant stimuli influences the results with the instrument. A typical group of subjects had an average grip of about 24 kilograms. When they smelled perfume the grip increased to 26, and when they smelled burnt hair or cheese it dropped to 22. The influence of the feelings may also be demonstrated in memory experiments. When the subjects studied ten nonsense syllables under standard conditions following the reading of either a pleasant or an unpleasant story, one and one-half more words, on the average, were remembered under the former condition. An extensive review of the literature on this point indicates general agreement that items which are either pleasant or unpleasant are learned more readily than those which lack this element. The superiority of the pleasant to the unpleasant from the standpoint of learning is not pronounced in this review, but the normal tendency to prolong pleasant experiences is an important consideration.

One of the most obvious ways in which to create a pleasant attitude toward the advertisement is to make it artistically attractive. This principle constitutes one justification of so-called "art for business' sake." There is some experimental evidence available to indicate that good art work is actually superior in attention or memory value to poor art work. Eight colored posters advertising a brand of coffee, all in car-card size, were displayed in university classrooms during an entire lecture hour. At varying time intervals after the initial display members of the classes were asked to write a description of the posters they could remember. A group of art teachers and professional artists had previously agreed on the two posters which were best and the two which were worst from an art standpoint. In the experiment 83 per cent of the former were recalled and only 29 per cent of the latter when the test was given immediately. A day later the corresponding figures were 71 per cent and 17 per cent. After 10 days the percentages were 57 and 12, after 20 days 50 and 11, and after 120 days 24 and 3. The posters which had been selected by experts as more artistic obviously made a greater impression on the group of laymen participating in the experiment. These results are in accord with the preceding discussion to the effect that pleasantness prolongs attention. Artistic elements may contribute to that pleasantness.

Lines

It is not feasible in a work of the present scope to consider all aspects of esthetics and artistic composition. A few points may be mentioned, however, which bear on the advertiser's problems. One of these deals with the fact that different types of lines are associated with certain feelings and may thus be used to lend atmosphere to the product advertised. Books on esthetics are replete with lists of qualities suggested by different kinds of lines. For instance the fine gray line is supposed to suggest delicacy and the fine black line precision and hardness, while the broad rough line carries an impression of homeliness and lends texture to the article. On that basis fine, gray lines might be used for advertising delicate lace, fine black lines for watches, and broad rough lines for camping supplies. Associations like the foregoing should not receive too much weight. Experimental evidence is lacking, and it is difficult to formulate a theoretical basis for them. In a few instances, however, certain qualities suggested by lines seem plausible and in some other cases experimental data are available. A few such cases will be discussed.

Direction. It is often asserted that vertical lines carry an atmosphere of simplicity, permanence, dignity, or rigor. This assertion has some theoretical plausibility because of association with towers and columns which rear themselves with a certain rigor and severity or with dignified persons who stand erect. The horizontal line suggests rest or quiescence plausibly enough because people frequently are seen resting in a horizontal position. The greater ease of eye movements in a horizontal direction may also be a factor. The diagonal line, in contrast to the horizontal or vertical is generally conceded to suggest action. When a person or animal is in action many diagonal lines are obvious to an observer, and an association of the diagonal with activity might readily be built up. Another principle which influences esthetic reactions is termed empathy. Etymologically this signifies "feel in" and denotes a tendency to project one's self into the object which he is contemplating. In looking at the picture of a landscape one feels himself into it and tends to do something such as walk among the trees. In the drama he may project himself into the situation and share the feelings of the persons on the stage or screen. Similarly, in looking at a mere diagonal line one may feel himself into the object, tip forward with the line and move so that he will not fall. If an object looks top-heavy the observer is inclined to jump in and, figuratively, push it back into position. Empathy might also operate in the attitude mentioned above with reference to horizontal or vertical lines. It should not be inferred that the observer necessarily goes through the motions described, but there may be a corresponding incipient motor adjustment.

Curves, in general, are conceded to be more pleasant than straight lines. It used to be thought that this tendency was due to the smooth movement with which the eye swept along the curve. Photographs of the eye movements when looking at curves reveal that this is not the case at all. The eye fixates one portion of the curve and then takes a short cut across in a straight line to another point. It is probable that the mechanism of empathy rather than eye movements accounts for the pleasantness of curves. The observer feels himself into the curve, going along it smoothly without any obstruction.

G. W. Ovink

Legibility, Atmosphere-value and Forms of Printing Types

1938. pp. 72-76

Recognition of Single Words

GESTALT FACTORS

If a character is assembled with other characters into a word, it loses its individuality so completely that only wilful visual abstraction can isolate it again. Standing isolated, the surrounding white space being background, its lines form a confined whole that cannot be brought into relation with its surroundings. But if it stands close to other characters, the space between the characters loses its background quality to some extent. For example: the right-hand outline of an isolated character has its principal meaning only in relation with the inside or the left-hand outline; standing next to the left-hand outline of another character, it can be regarded as the left-hand outline of the white space next to it. Under circumstances the outline as such is seen only in opposition to another figure beside it. Hence both the nature of the letterspace and the outline of the characters are of prime importance to the degree to which the single-character

Gestalten are suited for subordination under the new word-gestalt.

We observed in series I and II some letters falling to pieces, because a part of them had such a strong Gestalt, that the other parts could not be seen in relation to it. We wanted to make easily recognizable characters, i.e. strong Gestalten, but for that purpose we had to use parts of the strongest existing Gestalten, which consequently tried to restore themselves. Anthropomorphically speaking, they lived their own life before we forced them to play a subordinated role in new surroundings and now they try to become independent and to live their own old life again. Exactly the same view-point can be applied in regard to words.

The single character is a Gestalt of feebler structure than its components before their subordination, so again the word, which has a less strong Gestalt than its components (the single characters) originally had. And a very strong letter-gestalt does not want to be subordinated to the word-gestalt. Consequently the best form for isolated characters is the worst for use in word relation. This is the key to the problem of the relative legibility of roman versus sans-serif and also of roman versus Fraktur.

SPACE AND OUTLINE

Let us go back to letterspace and outline for a further substantiation.

Among the conditions promoting the creation of new Gestalten out of independent visual objects, have been found *nearness* and *equality*. So a group of scratches amidst other, but more widely scattered ones, will stand out as a Gestalt, and if in the same field some equally large circles are strewn, they will also detach themselves from the scratches as a pattern of their own.

Applied to our problem this means that no good word-gestalt is obtained if the characters are not well-fitted.

Therefore spacing forces us to spell, which means to read slowly and carefully. Too little space ultimately leads also to illegibility, because the characters must retain a certain degree of individuality. Similarity of the characters is promoted by similarities in the outline; if all the characters are built in a rectangle, such as the old Gothic 'Textur', they lose their individuality, and the result is illegibility. But maximal individuality is equally bad: the single characters cannot be subsumed under a whole. Those types are the best, that keep the *juste milieu* between individuality and equality.

BOLDNESS

There is another instance where the single characters remain too independent, and here we have bold types in mind. These are more visible, they call attention to themselves and that is reason enough to make them unsuitable for subordination. Moreover they have often less clear forms, because the necessary internal white space is consumed for the addition of weight. The lines come nearer to each other, which makes the occurence of 'short circuits', disintegration into simpler and stronger structures more frequent, as we saw in part I. Moreover irrelevant parts are more likely to be stressed.

The ordinary Bodoni editions have generally been found to be less legible, probably because of the combined effect of boldness and exclusively vertical stress; which does not lead on to the adjoining character. The general aspect of Bodoni can be much the same as of a 'Textur' page: the individual forms are lost in the multitude of verticals, because the equality makes a connection between all the latter ones.

Too thin characters often fail on the score of visibility, but if this is not the case, we must suppose that the white space in and around the thin lines lose their background character or, which is the same, that the lines of the figure become mere outlines, seen only in relation to the white planes of which they mark the borders. Here again, as with bold types, an approach to strokes of more uniform thickness is made; the result is that parts, which contribute little or nothing to recognition, receive relatively too much emphasis.

EXPERIENCE

In the word-gestalt not all parts stand on the same level of strength. Some of them (combinations of two or more characters, syllables, or even words, if they are used separately) are parts of many other words too. It will be clear that these parts have a tendency to separate themselves from the word-gestalt, if one keeps in mind what has been said of the Gestalt in relation with experience. On the other hand, if they are too strongly connected with the other parts in the new complex, they are apperceived more easily. This means that word-endings, such as -ably, -ously, -ingly, etc., receive but little attention because we focus directly on the stem, a circumstance which is the cause of many misreadings. For, if we give a word merely a cursory glance, because we recognize some parts of it and therefore take the meaning of the word for granted, it can easily happen that the unseen part is not the one expected. It takes some familiarity with the classical languages to be able not only to understand, but also to read quickly such composite words as incommensurability, irreducibility etc. The difficulty here is due, first, to the recognition *überhaupt* of these additional words as such. This recognition is partly founded upon knowledge of the entire addition, partly on conversance with the stems (e.g. -duci-, -versa-, -voca-, etc.) because the syllables of the stems mostly consist of a consonant plus vocal, which makes them look equivalent to ir-, re-, -bi, li, ty, whereas they should be taken together. Secondly, (but that is another problem) to the quantity of different vocals, which are not easily said in the silent pronunciation by which reading is accompanied. Where such a cumulation of the same or similar characters occurs, the attention is shifted from the total impression to the details, and that is where clear single characters are required. Always lack of knowledge of a word makes attention focus itself on detail, whereas command of the language makes it turn towards the whole.

Nothing could be more common than this, that we have a good look at something we must use without knowing it well. Another aspect gives the opposite; that we should not be continually forced to look intently at something we know quite well. Translated for our problem: for any text, that contains many common parts (i.e. well-known = good Gestalten) we should use a type that does not force itself upon us, but that reproduces the text in a simple conversational tone; for any text (be it half a page, or one word, or a line, or a row of figures) that does not contain parts that we can expect on the score of the logical development, or that we know well, we should use a type that presents us on its own initiative the whole thing cut and dried, clearly pronunciated. It is equally annoying to hear trivialities being presented as important novelties as to hear messages carelessly and casually bold, which one has eagerly awaited.

The problem of the relative legibility of printing-types can only be well understood after analysis of the reading attitude. We saw that a character that is eminently clear if isolated, cannot be subsumed easily in the word-complex. One next conclusion is, that apperceptive reading (interest directed on detail) requires another kind of type than assimilative reading, which needs an unobtrusive medium.

Otto Neurath

International Picture Language

1936. pp. 12-22

 ISOTYPE

International

System

Of

TYpographic

Picture

Education

The Question of an International Language

The desire for an international language is an old one, and it is more than ever in men's minds at this time of international connections in business and science. But 'debabelization' is a very hard and complex work. The attempt to make one international language has given us a parcel of new languages. The best way out seems to be the use of instruments which are, or have become, international. For this reason this book is in Basic English, because this international language is part of an old language in general use.

The question of an international language has now become important. There are a number of signs pointing to a great development of international organization in the near future —though we are living in a time of warring interests and broken connections. Any work done on the question of international languages—with a view to making a word language, or a helping picture language—will give support to international developments generally. An international language has to take into account international needs, and at the same time it has to be as simple as possible.

Every language is complex—even the simplest. Its store of words and its rules make it possible to put a statement into other words or one group of statements in the place of another. The words 'here' and 'now' may be used in talk, but in a book time and place are not common to the writer and the reader, so the book has to give the points of time and place in their relation to our general system of time and place. Statements are more or less clear-cut; the words used in business and talk are not as complete as they might be; when persons are face to face it is enough to give an idea of what is in one's mind if one's hearers are conscious what the question is. That is the same even with the language of science. The name of the book makes clear its range, and the range makes clear the sense of the words.

All this is true not only of our normal language, and the special instruments of business and science, but, with special changes, of picture languages, as international instruments specially designed for education and advertisement. The 'words' and 'statements' of the picture language—signs and their order—are not the same in pictures in a book as they are in pictures on walls. A special organization is necessary to make clear certain relations between them with the smallest possible number of words. Such adjustments to special purposes have to be made in any language.

To be good at a language more is needed than a knowledge of the words and of the rules: the sense of a word and of a group of words is different under different conditions. It is an art to get the full effect from the words. In the same way it is an art to get the full effect from pictures. To make a picture is a more responsible work than to make a statement, because pictures make a greater effect and have a longer existence. Every ISOTYPE picture is like a part of a great picture book or encyclopaedia, because all of them have to go together. This is necessary even with the pictures for boys and girls. The word language of boys and girls is not a special language but it is not complete. In the same sense the ISOTYPE language for a lower form of education is a part of the ISOTYPE language as a complete system in itself.

There are simple picture languages in which no other sorts of signs are used. What we have to do with here, however, is a picture language which is not able to give the story by itself, but only with the help of the words of a normal language.

Isotype as a Helping Language

In the Far East we see *one* language for writing, but a great number of languages for talking. We have made *one* international picture language (as a helping language) into which statements may be put from all the normal languages of the earth. We have given it the name 'ISOTYPE'.

A picture language of this sort is frequently very important and of great use. A man coming into a strange country without a knowledge of the language is uncertain where to get his ticket at the station or the harbour, where to put his boxes (see Picture 1), how to make use of the telephone in the telephone box (see Picture 2), where to go in the post office (see Picture 3). But if he sees pictures by the side of the strange words, they will put him on the right way. Signs might give the same sort of help in 'statistics' (making comparisons between amounts). The books of this science are full of numbers—the international signs of the language of mathematics—and words are only used to give their sense. But we

Where to put your boxes.

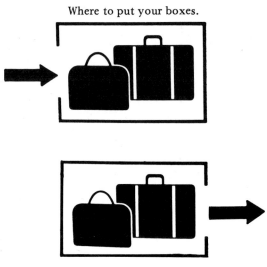

Where to get your boxes.

Picture 1.

are not able to get anything from them if we have no knowledge of the language used. A sign at the top of a list of numbers (see Picture 4) makes us almost independent of the knowledge of the language, because pictures, whose details are clear to everybody, are free from the limits of language: they are international. WORDS MAKE DIVISION. PICTURES MAKE CONNECTION.

Education by pictures in harmony with the ISOTYPE system, advertisement by ISOTYPE signs, will do much to give the different nations a common outlook. If the schools give teaching through the eye in harmony with this international picture language, they will be servants of a common education all over the earth, and will give a new impulse to all other questions of international education.

The ISOTYPE picture language is not a sign-for-sign parallel of a word language. It is a language which may be put into words in very different ways. The units of the picture language have different senses when they are in different positions.

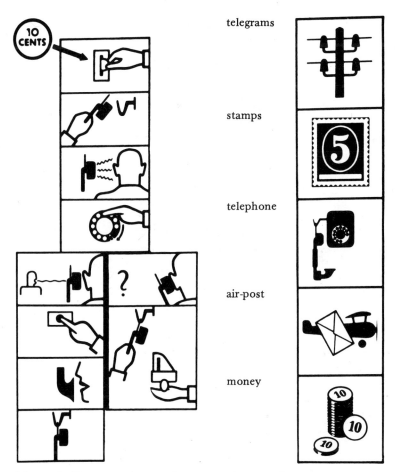

Picture 2. How to make use of
the telephone.

telegrams

stamps

telephone

air-post

money

Picture 3. Post-signs.

It is not possible to give a word for every part of such a picture or a statement for every group of parts. The parallel in
a normal language of a complete 'language picture' is a
complex group of statements; and an account in words of
what is in a group of language pictures would make a book.
The sense of every part of these pictures is dependent on the
sense of the complete picture and on its relation to the other

Gewerbebetriebe im Deutschen Reich 1933

	Betriebe	Männl. Beschäftigte	Weibl.
Bergbau usw	1 305	437 807	4 776
Eisen- und Stahlgewinnung	1 458	473 570	7 657
Herstellung v Eisen Stahl- u Metallwaren	155 833	492 694	92 952
Elektrotechnische Industrie	27 551	183 992	63 198
Chemische Industrie	7 699	182 443	63 986
Papierindustrie	10 886	118 936	62 171
Textilindustrie	67 579	385 840	460 991
Holz und Schnitzstoffgewerbe	214 640	555 179	52 638
Kautschuk und Asbestindustrie	1 948	27 775	20 519
Bekleidungsgewerbe	535 266	528 264	517 037

Picture 4.

parts of the picture. Like words they are used again and again
to make quite different statements.

Reading a picture language is like making observations
with the eye in everyday experience; what we may say
about a language picture is very like what we may say about
other things seen by the eye. For example: the man has
two legs; the picture-sign has two legs; but the word-sign
'man' has not two legs.

But the uses of a picture language are much more limited than those of normal languages. It has no qualities for the purpose of exchanging views, of giving signs of feeling, orders, etc. It is not in competition with the normal languages; it is a help inside its narrow limits. But in the same way as Basic English is an education in clear thought—because the use of statements without sense is forced upon us less by Basic than by the normal languages, which are full of words without sense (for science)—so the picture language is an education in clear thought—by reason of its limits.

Jacques Bertin

Sémiologie graphique

1967. pp. 6-8, translated by C. Ashwin

Resumé of General Theory—Definitions

Graphic representation constitutes part of the systems of signs which man has created in order to retain, understand and communicate observations which are necessary to him. Being a 'language' destined for the eye, it benefits from the properties of the ubiquity of visual perception. A monosemic system, it constitutes the rational part of the world of images.

In order to analyse it with precision it is necessary to distinguish it from musical, verabal and mathematical inscriptions, which are tied to temporal linearity; symbolism, which is essentially polysemic; and the moving image, which is dominated by the rules of cinematographic time. Within these strict limits, 'graphics' subsumes the world of graphs, that of diagrams, and the world of maps, which extends from the representation of atomic structures to the depiction of the galaxies, and embraces the world of plans and cartography.

Graphic representation derives its pedigree from its double function as an artificial memory and an instrument of research. A rational and effective tool when the characteristics of visual perception are fully employed, it constitutes one of the two 'languages' for the treatment of information. The cathode ray tube opens up for it a limitless future.

Definition of Graphic Representation

As a rational image, the graphic sign distinguishes itself from both the figurative and the mathematical image. In order to define it rigorously in relation to other systems of signs, the semiological approach has recourse to a combination of two kinds of evidence: a. the eye and the ear separate two kinds of systems; b. the significations which man attributes to signs can be monosemic, polysemic or pansemic.

THE MONOSEMIC SYSTEM

A system is monosemic when the knowledge of the signification of each sign *precedes* the observation of a combination of signs. An equation cannot be understood until the *unique* signification of each term has been established. A graphic representation cannot be understood until the unique signification of each sign has been established in accordance with the key. Conversely, a system is *polysemic* when the signification succeeds the act of observation and is deduced from the combination of signs. The signification is therefore personalised, and becomes *debatable*.

Consequently, a figurative image, and for example a photograph of something, or an aerial photograph, is always accompanied by a certain coefficient of ambiguity: who is this person? what is represented by this mark, this form? Faced with these questions, everyone can respond in his own way, for the interpretation is tied to the repertoire of analogies and the hierarchies of each 'receiver'. And one knows that this repertoire varies from one individual to another, according to personality, surroundings, period and culture. Before the polysemic image, the process of perception expresses itself with the question: 'This element, this combination of elements, what does it signify?', and perception consists of creating a code for the image. The work of the reader lies *between the sign and its signification.*

Signification attributed to signs	System of perception	
pansemic	MUSIC	NON-FIGURATIVE IMAGE
polysemic	WORDS	FIGURATIVE IMAGE
monosemic	MATHE-MATICS	GRAPHICS

Figure 1. The place of graphics in the systems of fundamental signs.

The non-figurative picture, that is to say the image which no longer signifies anything precise in order to attempt to signify 'everything', constitutes the 'pansemic' image, the extreme form of the polysemic.

By contrast, in graphic representation, and for example in a diagram or a map, every element is defined in advance. The process of perception is therefore very different, and consists of the question: 'Given that this sign signifies so-and-so, what are the relations established between all the signs, between all the things represented?' Perception consists of defining the relations which are established within the image or between images, or between the image and nature. The work of the reader is located *between the significations.*

This distinction is essential because it gives 'graphic representation' its whole meaning in relation to all other forms of visualisation. What does employing a monosemic system really mean? It means devoting a moment of consideration during which one attempts to reduce as far as possible the possibility of confusion, during which, in a certain context and during a certain period of time, *all the participants* agree upon certain significations, expressed by certain signs, and *agree not to debate them further.*

Hence this convention permits one to *discuss the collocation of signs* and to link together the propositions in a succession of factual statements, a succession which can then become 'non-debatable', that is to say 'logical'. This is the object of mathematics in systems which are tied to temporal linearity. It is the object of graphic representation in systems tied to the tridimensionality of spatial perception. On this point graphics and mathematics are alike, and construct the rational moment.

THE VISUAL SYSTEM

But graphics and mathematics differentiate themselves in terms of the perceptual structures which characterise them. It would need at least 20,000 successive instants of perception to compare two tables of figures of 100 lines in 100 columns. If the figures were transcribed into graphics the comparison would be very much easier, and could even be instantaneous.

In fact the perception of sound possesses no more than two sensory variables: the variation of sounds and their timing. All systems destined for the ear are linear and temporal. (We must remember that written transcriptions of music, words and mathematics are no more than formulae for memorising what are fundamentally sound systems, and that these formulae do not escape the linear and temporal character of these systems.)

	System of perception	
	🦻	👁
sensory variables	1. variation of sounds 1. variation of time	1. variation of marks 2. dimensions of layout
total	2 variables	3 variables
instantaneous perception	1 sound	Totality of relations of 3 variables

Figure 2. Perceptual properties of linear and spatial systems.

In contrast, visual perception employs *three* sensory variables: variation of mark, and the two dimensions of the plane surface, and these outside of time. The systems intended for the eye are at once spatial and atemporal. And this is the origin of their essential property: in an instant of perception linear systems cannot communicate to us more than *a single sound or sign*, whereas spatial systems, such as graphic representations, communicate in the same instant the *relations between three variables.*

To make best use of this considerable power of vision,

in the context of logical reasoning, such is the object of graphic communication, *the monosemic level of spatial perception.*

THE EVOLUTION OF GRAPHIC REPRESENTATION

The power of graphics has been recognised for a long time. The most ancient graphic representations which have been discovered are geographical maps engraved in clay, and they date probably from the third milennium BC. Graphic images were at first conceived, and are usefully still conceived, as reproductions of visible nature, and benefit from no more than one degree of liberty, namely that of the scale. In a molecular representation, in a geometric figure, a schematic montage, an industrial drawing, in a cross-section of land or a map, the two dimensions of the drawn plane correspond, according to scale, to visible space.

It was only in fourteenth-century Oxford that one catches a glimpse—confirmed by Charles de Fourcroy's discovery in the eighteenth century—that the two dimensions of a piece of paper could usefully represent *something other than visible space*. This was, in reality, to progress from simple representation to a complete 'system of signs' which was independent and possessed its own laws, that is to say its SEMIOLOGY.

And at the end of the twentieth century this system of signs reaches a new and fundamental stage as the result of the modern pressure of information and thanks to information theory. The main difference which one now sees between the graphic representation of the past, poorly differentiated from the figurative image, and the graphics of tomorrow, is the disappearance of the inherent fixity of the image.

Now that it has become manipulable by means of super-positions, juxtapositions, transformations, permutations, permitting groupings and classifications, the graphic image has been transformed from *the dead image* of 'illustration' to *the living image*, to an instrument of research accessible to all. Graphic representation is no longer only the re-presentation of a final simplification, it is also, and above all, *the definitive point of departure* and the instrument which permits the discovery and the defence of this simplification. Graphic representation has become as a result of its malleability an instrument for the treatment of information. Its study begins, therefore, with the analysis of the information to be transcribed.